D1558455

STUDIO MALKA

STUDIO MALKA

HABITATS OF THE XXIst CENTURY

GRAPHIC DESIGN **LAURENT GARBIT**
EDITORIAL DIRECTION **MELANIE MENDELEWITSCH**
CONSULTANT RENDERINGS **TRISTAN SPELLA**
PHOTOGRAPHERS **LAURENT CLEMENT** - **LAURENT GARBIT** - **STEPHANE MALKA**

NEW YORK

New York · Paris · London · Milan

Through the works and research of the French firm Studio Malka Architecture, this book aims to showcase a panel of groundbreaking and innovative contemporary habitats. This framework of reflections seeks to create architectural alternatives adapted to our current, and emerging, ways of living.

Major events have occurred all around the globe in the twenty-first century, starting with the 2008 economic crisis that shook the foundations of the financial system, immediately and directly impacting the housing sector. More recently, the years of 2020 and 2021 were marked by the global COVID-19 pandemic. Public spaces have been deserted in unprecedented ways, and houses have been fully reinvested. We are witnessing a conscious, massive, and symbolic appropriation of our homes, which architects must support.

Let's face it: the habitat, as we knew it in developed countries, is no longer a relevant model; the pandemic has made people around the globe finally realize that effective work can be done remotely, thanks to wireless technologies.

New needs regarding the hybridization of housing are now growing, including an increased demand for home offices and the necessity of new layers of privacy inside the house itself.
On a larger scale, the post-COVID-19 world accelerated the metropolitan exodus, along with the desire to reconnect with ourselves and with nature via a temporary or a more permanent and sustainable getaway.

Some of us may choose a radical solution by living off the grid, alone or along with a community of will.

Meanwhile, in cities, new urban strategies have been developed by building vertically, aiming to fit the skylines and the horizon with effective solutions and fast, green construction. As a result of this new era of remote work, workspaces have been left behind, requiring the necessary adaptation of those spaces.

Since the 1990s, offices have been designed with an increasing desire for a "home away from home" feeling, integrating domestic services such as kitchens, showers, salons, and even rooms for sleeping.

The offices and shops that Studio Malka Architecture have produced are fully flexible and involve various modular spaces. They can easily be modified without any additional construction or demolition into housing that fulfills the needs of the post-pandemic era.

The guidelines of this new architecture are based on the premise of extending what exists without destroying it, transforming the old by adding a new urban layer.

The book is divided into four chapters, focusing on four main types of contemporary habitats:

GETAWAYS
Revealing the embedded architecture. Underlining heritage and the local savoir faire while merging influences and invoking different cultures, with a consistent link to vernacular architecture.

While the concepts of travel and mobility have always fueled the architectural imagination, they are more essential than ever in times of confinement and remote working.
By prioritizing habitat over location, this chapter explores the feeling of escape provided by architecture, a vector of motionless journeys that give full meaning to the term "home."

OFF THE GRID
Downsizing habitats. Creating conscious community shelters, architectural "guerilla spaces", mobile housing. Inhabiting the thickness of a wall to extend the limits of public space.

In an era that is ultra-connected to the point of becoming anxiety-provoking, silence and reconnection to the natural elements are the ultimate luxury. From the Nevada to the Sahara Desert, from the cave dwellings of Santorini to Jerusalem, above a Parisian bridge or in a house immersed in the wild, this chapter is an overview of nested projects designed as architectural refuges.

OFF THE GROUND
Blurring the distinctions between art and architecture, using urbanity as a political weapon. Para-siting the city, literally leaning on it, developing new urban strategies and new sustainable alternatives. Hijacking existing materials as architectural ready-mades, injecting life on facades and rooftops to create an architectural Kama Sutra.

How should we (re)learn to breathe in an increasingly suffocating urban environment?
This chapter explores alternative ways to rehabilitate cities and gather people thanks to the infinite possibilities offered by vertical uprising architecture, and the contemporary rediscovery of a centuries-old European architectural process that provides the discovery of new and unexpected horizons, even in the vibrant heart of the city.

FLEXIBLE FUTURE
Interconnecting modular spaces with the use of "mutant" furniture, escaping the matrix through polymorphic spaces and floating, moving walls. Dissolving space limitations with stealth camouflage and chromatic architecture.

Throughout the twentieth century, designed workspaces were a succession of failures; because space planning never gave any thought to improvisation, workspace trends had to change every decade. We came to realize that factories, designed for machines, turned out to be the best version of a modern habitat. Office spaces are often alienating, stressful places.
How to think about the future of architecture in our time of perpetual change? Versatile, flexible, and multifunctional, the architecture of tomorrow takes the existing iteration as its base and transforms it to adapt to new uses.

01 GETAWAYS

02 OFF THE GRID

03 OFF THE GROUND

04 FLEXIBLE FUTURE

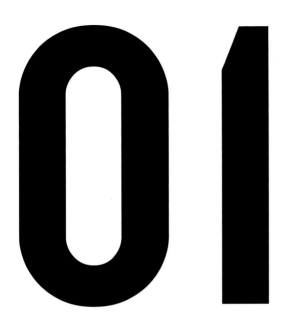

GETAWAYS

CHEOPS OBSERVATORY

NECROPOLIS OF GIZA I EGYPT

Framing the Great Pyramid

The Cheops Observatory is an artist's residence, a gateway at the entrance of the desert, an inhabited belvedere a short walking distance to the largest of the pyramids of Giza. Located on the plateau of the Giza Necropolis, the project is nestled in the village of Nazlet-el-Samaan. This ancient site was founded in the seventh century by desert tribes fascinated by the pyramids; the village is a landmarked site and a journey through time; the most common transport is still by horse or camel. Restoring this village creates a bulwark against the massive tourist influx and real estate speculation so prevalent in these historical districts.

We worked with a systemic approach on informal architecture, on which an intervention was necessary for safeguarding and preserving the site's historical importance.

Following centuries-old oral traditions, the residence was built without any plans, using sketches drawn in the desert sand. Local construction techniques, application of ancestral knowledge, and crafts by the villagers were an essential part of the project, underscoring its social and environmental commitment.

Materials were upcycled, diverted, and reused in a short circuit. Facades were made up of an accumulation of raw earth bricks, and recycled traditional windows and shutters came from the circular economy of the village. Part of the crowning consists of a triangular tent handcrafted by an ancestral tribe living in the Giza Desert.

A vertical stratification inscribes this architecture in a temporal process linking the vernacular, the contemporary, and the nomad in one main building. This architecture, with its variable geometry, allows both specific and integral protection, effective against the sun's rays, as well as optimal cooling air flow on all levels. The Observatory was built in an alignment with the Pyramid of Khufu (also known as the Pyramid of Cheops or the Great Pyramid of Giza), the oldest, largest, and the only one of the seven wonders of the ancient world still existing today.

The building has an east-west orientation, the optimal position to contemplate the trajectories of the sun and the moon. This exceptional site allows the examination of the relationship of the Pyramid to the North Star and the procession of the equinoxes. These relationships helped to create an architectural and landscape composition with logical continuities and concordances of views while opening impressive vistas toward the Pyramid from the garden, the swimming pool, the Time Room, and even on reflections on the furniture. The Time Room is a powerful and meditative observation space facing the Great Pyramid of Cheops. A wooden framework with pyramidal truss and radiating lines was designed in a new typology, allowing the height of the ceiling to be doubled. This triangular shape creates a three-dimensional portal that frames the Great Pyramid of Giza. The textile roof folds and unfolds very quickly and, depending on the season, creates an open, covered, or uncovered room. In addition, a horizontal canopy was installed on the west facade and the sunset creates a second irradiated anamorphosis of the great Pyramid of Khufu which is revealed in the center of the Time Room.

We designed a series of unique pieces of furniture to activate the different spaces of the Observatory. DELTA, both modular and multifunctional, can be used as tables of different lengths and heights, but also as chairs, shelves, polymorphic sculptures, and even as beds. Triangles allow a multiplicity of combinations. Built to be used in a very flexible way, these pieces can be reversed and combined together three-dimensionally, allowing everyday objects to perform different tasks. The design of this furniture features the four elemental glyphs: Fire, Water, Air, and Earth, creating a blend of triangular purity connected to the Great Pyramid of Cheops. Activated depending on how the piece has been assembled, these glyphs invoke various fundamental alchemical symbols found within the Giza Necropolis.

Connected to the elements, this architecture opens out without artifices, bays, glazing, or other dividers to enjoy a dynamic relationship with its environment, generating a hypercontextual space, at once sensory and porous. The Cheops Observatory is both open and closed, nomadic and sedentary, masculine and feminine construction. Back to the basics of architecture, it creates a dialogue between local vernacular architecture and an architectural ready-made, and an answer to the necessary evolution of informal architecture, one of the fundamental issues of the twenty-first century.

GOLDEN CITY

PARIS I FRANCE

Revealing Intangible Spaces - Stacking Territories

Golden City is collective housing for Egyptian students in Paris's Citè Internationale Universitaire. Also known as "La Maison d'Egypte," this building aims to be an emblematic vector of Egyptian culture, which is a rich blend of both Arabic and African influences. To understand all those multiple identities, we need to go back in time and travel to Egypt's predynastic period, when the land was inhabited by tribal groups and autonomous clans. Progressively, these territorial ruptures would become multiple Sepats, lately called Nomes by the Greeks.

These Nomes were the administrative districts of Ancient Egypt; Upper and Lower Egypt had a total of 42 Nomes registered until the Ptolemaic period. In these provinces there is, for example, the Nome of the White Wall (Memphis, Saqqarah), the Nome of Scepter (Thebes), the Nome of the Country of Nubia (whose principal cities are Philae, Elephantine, Kom Ombo), the Nome of the Fortress (Nekhen, El Kab) amongst others.

The genesis of the project was born from the desire to embrace this complexity. By thinking of the project as federation of different identities, we created a physical and symbolic representation of the forty-two provinces of ancient Egypt; the building features forty-two megalithic prefabricated blocks representing the unique breadth of Egyptian identity.

The concept is defined in a transversal way throughout the experience; within the building, we aim to transliterate an interior territorial landscape where each province is represented by its respective local crafts, furniture, sculpture, and decorative arts. Lighting, graphic identity, objects, and paintings are specific to each of the areas, and each is provided with its own totemic emblem: falcon, crocodile, cobra, gazelle, sycamore, etc.

Golden City is not a single building, but rather a functional superposition of territorial spaces, created with extra-large prefabricated blocks that aggregate and federate.

It is a representation of a new Egyptian identity in France, one at the crossroads of ancient history and modern culture, using physical, mystical, and timeless architecture. It is a journey through the regions and provinces of Egypt and also through time, where history and mythology merge with the most contemporary uses.

INSTITUT DU MONDE ARABE

PARIS I FRANCE

Inhabiting a Matriarchal Architecture

"Throughout history, women handled the haima. In a physical way, first. To weave, sew, maintain, assemble, disassemble the tent. Women and community. This is the *tuisa*, a tent that can support more than two hundred pounds. One year for the weaving, ten hands to sew it, twenty hands to carry it. … They give the weave a solid texture, impervious to the cold of the night and winter, and heat from the most intense sun."
—Christiane Perregaux, *Women of the Desert*

Installed in front of L'Institut du Monde Arabe's museum by the River Seine in the very heart of Paris during the *Contemporary Morocco* exhibition, this gigantic tent is an innovative interpretation of the traditional Saharawi tent. Entirely handwoven from camel and goat wool in the traditional way by a cooperative of Moroccan women, this flexible artwork covers a surface of five thousand square feet.

Easily assembled and disassembled by nomadic peoples during their desert journeys throughout Morocco, this type of soft architecture is an ephemeral and mobile installation, where height variations give a topographical and territorial dimension.

This contemporary tent combines history and technical innovation, while creating a large, free-access space hosting a literary/coffee place, a performance space, a design store, and an exhibition of contemporary Moroccan handicrafts.

It is a tribute to the ancient peoples of the desert as well as an experimental mutation of these Bedouin tents, where their history preserved while expanding their architectural vocabulary. Thanks to its woolen cloth, our tent is a blend of organic, rough, dense, almost living architecture. This installation creates a sensual face-to-face conversation between Jean Nouvel's solid glass-and-steel facade and a matriarchal, flexible, furry architecture.

LE FLIG EST ASSOCIÉ
À UNE MEMBRANE ÉTANCHE
QUI PERMET À L'OUVRAGE DE
RÉSISTER À DES CONDITIONS
RADICALEMENT DIFFÉRENTES
DE SON ENVIRONNEMENT HABITUEL.
TENDUE SUR DOUZE MÂTS DE
HAUTEURS VARIABLES,
CETTE STRUCTURE,
À UN RYTHME TOPOGRAPHIQUE
ET UNE DIMENSION TERRITORIALE.

LE FLIG A VOYAGÉ
DES COOPÉRATIVES DE FEMMES
DU MAROC SAHARIEN
À DES ATELIERS BRETONS DE CONFECTION
POUR EN PERMETTRE LA PRÉPARATION
À SON INSTALLATION.

80 BANDES TISSÉES DE 17 M DE LONG
PAR 0,5 M ONT ÉTÉ PRÉPARÉES
POUR COUVRIR LES 680 M² D'INSTALLATION

LE FLIG EST UN CAMPE
QUI REGROUPE PL
- KHAYMAS - QUI
D'USAGES DIFFÉRENTES, D'HAB
OU DE PRO

TANTAN NANTES   KHAYMAS F

COP22'S ARK

MARRAKECH I MOROCCO

Emergency Climatic Architecture

Designed for COP22's United Nations Climate Change Conference in Marrakech, our approach with the Ark22 project is set at the crossroads between a light architecture masterwork and monumental art installation.

Located at the former main entrance to Marrakech's medina, this site is in the Valley of Ourika and at the foot of the Atlas Mountains.

Ark22 is a gate between the desert and the city, embodying the supporting role of architecture to the environment. The project highlights the singular within the whole, emphasizing the importance that each of our actions has on the environmental disasters we are now facing. To reflect this idea, the structure is composed of over ten thousand identical raw wooden boards collected from local, sustainably managed forests, and is designed to generate regulated airflow inside the building. It is a pointillist accumulation of embedded wood timbers, built without nails or screws.

Ark22 explores the limits of Gestalt theory in architecture. The project's arches are built by both the physical and the immaterial, by presence and absence; in fact, our brain attempts to simplify and organize these complex vertical stackings by analyzing it subconsciously as a monumental arch. Our intellect automatically draws the lines between solids and voids to create the general form of the whole nonexistent figure. Therefore, the project has a different physical presence depending where it is viewed from; as the viewer approaches, the gigantic baroque mass breaks down to reveal the minimal modular units.

In order to have a neutral carbon footprint, all the materials used are reused and upcycled. In fact, they were merely temporarily diverted from their ultimate destination; after the conference, the wood timber was dismantled and rebuilt as a kindergarten in Marrakech.

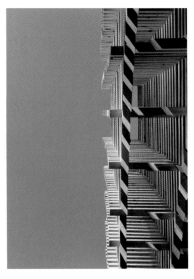

MUGU HOUSE

MALIBU CALIFORNIA I USA

Inhabiting the Hills

Located at Mugu Point, California, fifty miles from Los Angeles, the Mugu House is embedded in Malibu's steep cliffs.

The residence takes advantage of the existing topography and porosities of the site.

The result is zero impact on the surrounding area, an ecological project immersed in and connected to the natural environment. This lightweight architecture uses prefabricated alveolar concrete made from primary locally available materials, such as sand and aggregates, with a very low (seven percent) cement content. This composition reduces carbon dioxide emissions by twenty-eight times compared with traditional concrete. Easy to build and to remove, this project allows a quick, inexpensive, clean, sustainable, and waste-free installation. Built with very few partitions, the rock determines the geometry of the interior spaces; the flank of the uninterrupted mountain extends inside each room, reminding us that we are guests of nature. The Mugu House embodies a return to the roots of architecture connected with the natural elements, a dialogue with the mountain and its naturally formed caves.

The house is in constant conversation with its surroundings: its lichens, succulents, and other vegetation.

Thanks to large bay windows, on looking out, one is made to feel as a part of the ocean, fully immerged in it, inviting the California panorama as part of the house.

The double-skin facade is composed of removable triangular units, generating different types of solar patterns through a series of wooden sunscreens based on Amerindian tribal patterns.

The architecture of the Mugu House links both nature and history, sustainability and permanence: the house revisits the original shelter trope by creating a vernacular dialogue with the mountain, and embodies a return to the roots of the American continent.

CASA LLUNA

MALLORCA BALEARIC ISLANDS I SPAIN

Revealing the Heritage

Located in the Balearic Island of Mallorca in Sa Pobla, on the remote northern part of the island between agriculture areas, preserved ecosystems, and crystal-clear coves, Casa Lluna was originally built in 1947 as a corral, an extension of a village farmhouse.

Stéphane Malka was not only the lead architect but also the owner of the house. "During one of my trips around the Mediterranean Sea, I stumbled upon Mallorca, almost by accident. I was immediately struck by its powerful natural light and the majestic nature of this island. This Balearic sun temple brought back reminiscences of my native South of France's landscapes, a 'hyper-Provence' exotic and yet familiar, sharing the same Mediterranean culture that I am bound to." The approach of the project was to preserve the Mallorcan heritage as much as possible while utilizing clever interventions when necessary.

The ground floor is developed around formal and informal working spaces: a patio, an exhibition space, and a wellness area. Malka's wellness routine includes exercises, yoga, and meditation. As he is an avid swimmer, the patio also includes a saltwater pool equipped with a counter-current swimming lane, a unique cross-training system he has developed and patented, a hydromassage system devoted to Watsu sessions. The wellness zone also includes an indoor infrared sauna. This area is covered with a roof but bears no glass windows or door in order to connect with the natural rhythm of the air flow and Mallorca's very specific seasonal scents.

The first floor is dedicated to reception, with a one thousand square foot area accommodating a large living room, a lounge with a fireplace, and a dining area connected to an open kitchen.

A large terrace links to the patio, and guest rooms and balconies are also connected. Totally self-sufficient, the house is powered by solar panels, and the pool is filled with filtered rainwater. The rainwater is directed from the roof to the capacious antique Moorish pear-shaped well that was built centuries before the house, purified through reverse osmosis, and pressurized to provide drinking water.

Casa Lluna features raw, uncoated, breathable, and organic sustainable materials, and the aesthetic, throughout the house, reflects the aesthetic of the essential, an authentic approach of a traditional Balearic farmhouse.

The house showcases various installations, injecting modernity in this traditional Mallorcan dwelling. Hidden inside a former closet, for example, is a long and narrow Jack-and-Jill bathroom with infinite reflections, separating a guest room and a studio. Mirror installations were set in various locations, while mobile mirrored walls were designed to separate the different areas when needed, while also extending natural light, shifting perspectives, and stretching seemingly impossible views along the walls.

DUNK HOUSE

MANHATTAN BEACH CALIFORNIA I USA

Hybride & Stealth Architecture

The Dunk House was created for a former NBA basketball player based in Los Angeles County's Manhattan Beach.

Born from the fusion of basketball and architecture, the Dunk House is equipped with a courtyard boasting a full-size basketball court fully integrated in the building itself. The court is open to the city, in the great tradition of streetball.

The architecture is composed of two simple shifted blocks, one compact toward the street and the other wide open over the garden.

The villa merges color and materiality to develop a contemporary stealth camouflage approach; Studio Malka Architecture created the L.A.B. (Los Angeles Blue) color.

This polarized blue paint interacts with the various solar luminosities and automatically adjusts its color to match the Californian sky's tones, merging the house with its surroundings.

In the backyard, a fully mirrored guest house reflects the sun's rays on the shaded north facade of the house, causing both the total "disappearance" of the guest house and the embodiment of the main house via reflections.

The result is a contextual alliance between the very materiality of the house and its surroundings, proactively interacting with the streets of LA, the beach community, the sun's latitude, and the sky's intensity.

KEMER VILLAS

ANTALYA I TURKEY

Modernity Meets Vernacular

The Mediterranean Sea, the cobalt blue line, is not just an identity but a journey in itself.

For this project, we drew from the deep roots of the local Mediterranean culture, with its Persian, Ottoman, and Byzantine influences, to create architecture that is elegant and sophisticated, and also minimal and contemporary.

The result is a series of interconnected eco-housing units of distinct, pure white masses, in the great tradition of the Turkish coastal cities, such as the old city of Izmir with its traditional whitewash architecture, and the hanging houses on Bodrum's hills.

The geometric forms feature bleached wood lattices that filter the light and materialize architecture by creating thin shadows.

Our goal was to reinvent Turkish modernity by revisiting vernacular architecture, using local resources, materials, and thermal waters.

This concept is adhered to throughout the entire experience, from architecture to furniture and lights, and from branding and tableware to, of course, food.

All of the furniture is made by local artisans, and the driftwood pieces bring natural and authentic touches to the spaces, and recall the original meaning of Mediterranean: between sea and land. The wood and whitewash create a rhythm to the sensorial experience of the rooms, while the elaborate vines and tree stumps are re-worked through a contemporary prism. Additional outdoor showers, open to the sky, reframe the preserved natural landscape, continuing the harmonious experience with nature.

In this project, we aimed to bring a new approach, between tradition and modernity, by selecting the best of both, and opening new horizons to create dreamlike and timeless architecture.

VILLA LENA

TUSCANY I ITALY

Inhabiting the Canopy

Villa Lena is a unique creative agritourism experience located in the wilds of Tuscany. Set on five hundred hectares of hillside olive groves, vineyards, vegetable gardens, and woodland, this complex includes a hotel, an organic farm, an art foundation with artists' residences and studios, and a newly-built multi-story wellness retreat center as close to nature as it gets. All resources are local; the building is made with wood and bamboo taken from the hill on which it sits. By knitting bamboo together, we created a porous surface, open to the air and light, creating on the walls and facades a lively claustra with ever-changing, filtered views.

The foundation is built on the voids of old dry dwells, allowing the building to have no impact on the soil. Atop the property's highest hill, this retreat provides a unique view toward the ancient pilgrimage route of Santiago de Compostela and the crossroads of the ten Tuscan provinces.

BUNGALOW TECH

PRASLIN I SEYCHELLES ISLANDS

Inhabiting Nature

Located on the island of Praslin in the Seychelles, in a nature reserve proclaimed a World Heritage Site by UNESCO in 1983, this project of eco-lodges treads softly on the land.

Working with Philippe Starck Network, we proposed a master plan of structures on studs, elevated from the ground so as not to impact their surroundings and whose decks float on the island's existing vegetation. The offsite construction of the prefabricated habitats allows a superficial installation on site, without having to dig any foundations. The lodges are strictly made out of natural low-tech materials, such as renewable and recyclable wood, mud, and lime, and materials diverted and reused, such as corrugated metal sheets. The island is further engaged by collecting rainwater and using soft techniques to purify wastewater. Local construction techniques are used, and the local community's craftsmanship is reflected in the project, bringing together both social and environmental commitment. The reception rooms have a roof covered by peat, cinnamon, and wild orchids that allow visual and olfactory pleasure while optimal insulation is created by using solid hardwoods in the living rooms. The pervasiveness, sometimes to the point of intrusion, of the local flora gives the sensation of living in a protected environment within the mangrove. This strategy allows nature to invigorate architecture, to enhance it by progressively leaning more and more on it, turning it slowly into a contemporary habitable ruin, reconnecting the bonds between nature and culture.

02

OFF THE GRID

LOOPCAMP
BURNING MAN

NEVADA I USA

Architectural Ready-Made

A loop is a musical sequence, a sound circle; Loopcamp is a hybrid of housing and an organic musical instrument.

It is a camp too, a shelter against Nevada's frequent storms at the Burning Man festival. With the festival arises a spontaneous city of eighty thousand inhabitants settled on ancient Native American lands near the now-dry Lahontan Lake, seven hundred feet above sea level.

Black Rock City is the last social utopia since the creation of Israel's first kibbutz. The temporary town is made of alternative visionary art and architecture such as capsules, geodesic domes, robots, balloons, art-cars, mobile homes and various installations, along with myriad electronic sounds.

With its post-industrial feeling and freewheeling environment, it recalls Archigram's avant-garde drawings, specifically *Instant City*, in a contemporary way.

Loopcamp is on the playa, where the central zone of the housing plan is completely open to the desert.

Disc-shaped city, round temple, and circular tubes: the trinity of city, building, and material is gathered around the loop to welcome the sandstorms. Oriented to face the direction of major winds, the shelter is composed of recycled paper tubes, slightly beveled to create sounds triggered by air pressure.

The shelter results from tubes of various lengths and widths, producing a spectrum of melodies and sounds; treble from short tubes, and bass from long tubes.

Based on a circular plan, Loopcamp radiates surround-sound with different tones depending on the winds, creating a unique and constantly reinvented sonar experience, and a physical translation of movement in the city and of the elements.

THE GREEN MACHINE

SAHARA DESERT

Greening the Desert

Commissioned for the Venice Architecture Biennale in 2014, The Green Machine is a mobile oasis, designed to green the desert. With the horizon in constant view, the desert fascinates with the magnificence of its landscapes and the purity of its lines. Beyond the silence and the visual appeal of this sublime landscape of absence, the desert is a territory rich in untapped resources. The potential influence of the desert on the surface of the globe is considerable; there are over fifteen million square miles of uncultivated desert land.

Seen through the prism of world overpopulation and global warming, the desert is a potential ally in terms of sustainability and human development. Every year, forty-six thousand square miles of land, equivalent to the size of Benin, is lost because of desertification and degradation. These territories could produce twenty million tons of cereal a year. The desertification of these lands creates famine, decreases food safety, and contributes to poverty in the region, damaging the economic stability of nomadic and farming communities. Poor land means poor people, political problems, and social unrest. Agriculture represents a fundamental building block of civilization; when biodiversity is lost, the entire social system goes bankrupt.

In 2007, the United Nations decreed desertification as one of the major issues of the twenty-first century. Indeed, territories and desert regions represent more than forty percent of the earth's surface, and sixty percent of earth meadows are becoming depopulated. The stakes in the Sahara Desert are regional, but also global. When the meadows are damaged, they release carbon into the atmosphere. The desert moves forward only when naked grounds are not covered, even slightly, with plants. Saharan grounds are directly subjected to strong climatic variations, hot until dusk and freezing at night until dawn. A simple vegetable litter would temper these ravaging variations on the ground level to modify the microclimate, and thus give one more large scale to the microclimatic land.

Thanks to holistic management and strategically placed grassland, it is possible to regenerate dry and semi-dry ground, beginning with the Saharan border and existing oases. Given that only twenty percent of the Saharan surface is a sand desert, the range of possibilities is wide. Joining this axis, the mobile Green Machine oasis is a platform—a nomadic and autonomous agricultural and industrial city of regeneration of deficient ecosystems and development of the permaculture. It's an ark of protection.

The structural slab of the city is raised on four Caterpillar Crawlers, originally designed to carry NASA rockets from the manufacturing plant to the launching pad, and which can be driven with a considerable load on any type of ground. The mobile oasis takes advantage of the hostile elements of the Saharan desert; the powerful sun and winds and great differences between daytime and nighttime temperatures. The Green Machine is autonomous in its use of power, and actually generates electricity and produces water.

The Green Machine oasis is equipped with low-tech systems such as:

* Nine floating balloons which produce 450m^3 of water daily from air condensation have the capacity to collect drinkable water from the air. The balloons collect steam from the air and liquefies it via condensation, to make it circulate in the vertical pipes to a reservoir placed on the slab. The same balloons are equipped with turbines which generate some renewable energy.
* Nine solar towers which produce 450 kilowatts of power every day.
* Twenty-four fields of wheat, five-thousand

square feet each, directly transformed in factories dedicated to the Saharan seeding.
* Four hydroponic agricultural greenhouses, each five thousand square feet.
* Four 700m^3 gallon water tanks.
* Livestock breeding and farms feed the inhabitants and fertilize the earth, inhabitants are fed and the local population are supplemented. Solid and liquid organic waste (after methanization and composting), fermentable waste, and waste water are recycled in a short local loop.
* Housing, schools, restaurants, places of relaxation, and pleasure gardens are included in the city.
* A retention pond of 50,000m^3.

The principle of revitalization of lands is simple and has already begun; thanks to the tilling of the earth by the Caterpillars, furrows were formed. The first pairs of Caterpillars allow a first ploughing on which is poured a contribution of water to move the earth and rock is mixed in the sand. Then, the next pair of Caterpillars inject a mixture of water, natural fertilizer, and cereal seeds. The ground is ready to absorb and to retain the water by storing

the carbon and by destroying the methane. On a longer timescale, the biodiversity develops:
* One year after a field is left uncultivated, it is colonized by seasonal plants that last for a year. Wildlife is limited to insects and small animals which pass by looking for seeds.
* Five years later, some shrubs and long-lasting herbaceous plants appear, but most of the plants are still short-lived. Also found are termite mounds and rodent dens.
* In ten years, long-lasting weeds are present and trees begin to grow. Jackals and hares hide among shrubs. Finally, the old field distinguishes itself as more than an oasis, and many sorts of plants and animals are present.

According to Allan Savory, researcher and developer of holistic farming techniques, if we could re-green half of the desert borders and the meadows of the world, the carbon preserved in the land would allow us to return to the environmental state of the preindustrial era, while feeding all of humanity.

BLVCK PYRVMID

NECROPOLIS OF GIZA I EGYPT

Expressing the Golden Ratio

Located in the Giza Necropolis archeological site, a pyramid was built in the twenty-first century. Studio Malka rebuilt the legendary Black Pyramid that disappeared from the Giza plateau. It is a mastaba, the original form of the step pyramid from the ancient Egyptian empire. The Black Pyramid, soon to be adorned with granite in the traditional method, is a tribute to architects Imhotep and Hemiunu; it is now the thirteenth pyramid erected on the Giza plateau. It is built according to the golden ratio, an omnipresent proportion used in the construction of the Cheops Pyramid, and also found throughout nature, from microscopic plant growth to the structure of the arms of the Milky Way. The Pyramid is connected to groundwater and may, depending on the season, be fully immersed by water, just like the first Egyptian temples of the Nile Valley; indeed, the pyramid is in a part of a basin and a plantation, facing west and the setting sun. Designed as a contemporary oasis, this micro-city is destined to welcome nomadic people and animals in the desert of the plateau. This pyramid is an inverted one, because the highest degree of this pyramid is on the same level as the ground, thus conferring a connection to the earth and beings rather than strictly to the sky.

A-KAMP47

MARSEILLE I FRANCE

Inhabiting the Walls - Reclaiming the City

The rapid shelter opens like an umbrella for urban campers searching for protection.

The illegitimate child of the minimal "unité d'habitation" of Le Corbusier and Claude Parent's "oblique housing environment," A-Kamp47 vertical camp is placed at La Friche de La Belle de Mai in Marseille, on a wall between a cultural center and a railroad network. These spaces are in legal ambiguity, balancing between private and public property. By appropriating blind walls, we are neither inside nor outside. This interstitial space has been taken and thickened in its verticality, like a corridor carved in between.

According to the Quiliot law of June 22, 1982, "to guarantee the right to housing constitutes a duty of solidarity for the entire nation." However, no law provides a national obligation for housing, and despite political promises, cardboard shelters and campsites under bridges are multiplying.

In the wealthier neighborhoods of Marseille, the homeless are installing themselves more visibly on front lawns, and squatting has become more common.

In the winter of 2006, the Children of Don Quichotte set up more than a hundred tents along the banks of the Canal St-Martin.

A logical evolution of lightweight shelters, the tent is mobile, but is subject to exposure to the elements, and also to theft and police raids. In this project, stealth shelters respond to the constraints of precarious social systems. The location of the site allows for a collective response.

The unhoused are sheltered.

The blind walls now have eyes, and they are watching us.

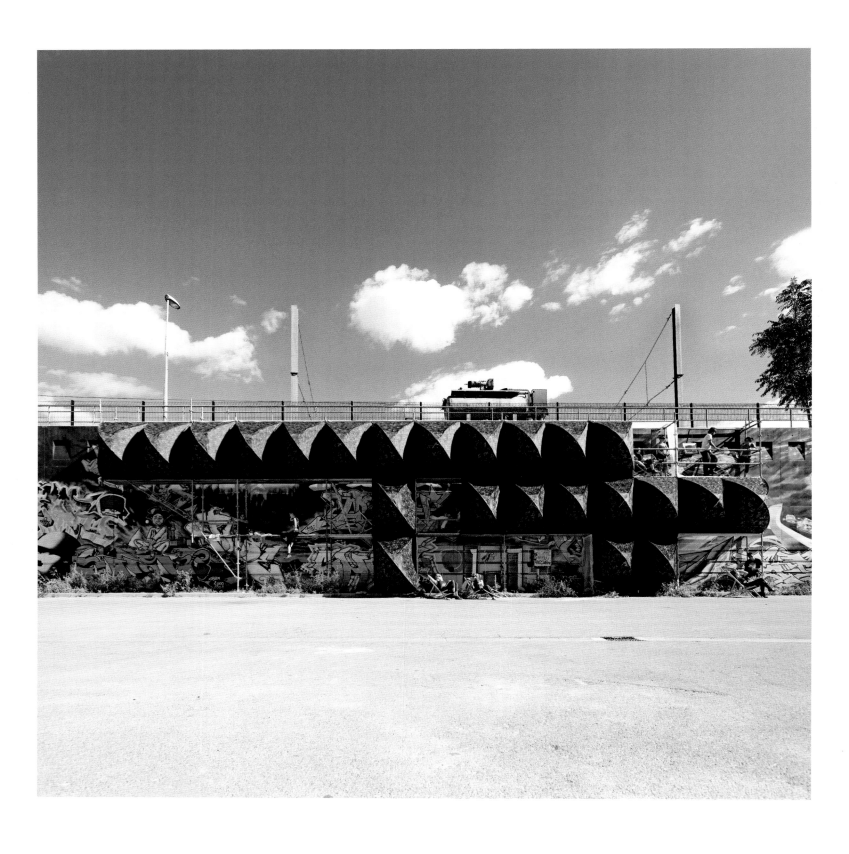

SELF DEFENSE

PARIS LA DEFENSE I FRANCE

Inhabiting the Walls - Architectural Guerilla

Determined to create a new social scenario, the Pocket of Active Resistance (PAR) system is a modular complex providing alternative habitation for lifestyles of defiance, positioning itself in a permanent state of insurrection. Its growth is articulated by the vitality of its spontaneous community.

A pocket of active resistance created by welcoming the discontented, this act of guerrilla architecture sets out to hijack the Great Arch of Fraternity to unite the forsaken, the marginalized, refugees, demonstrators, dissenters, hippies, utopians, and the stateless.

Since the creation of La Defense in 2009, world events such as Arab Spring, Occupy Wall Street, and the indignation movement in Europe attest to the embryonic development of a new social order. Outraged by society's unbridled capitalism, thousands of defiant citizens are occupying public spaces around the world. These are the foundations instigating a global "alter-socius," uniting people toward a common ideal.

Often dislodged, the PAR is a system that takes over public spaces, or in the case of La Grande Arche of La Defense, creates a compact and solid structure to resist police action. The primary function of the facade is to protect against external dangers; a front against batons, a shelter against tear gas.

The Pocket of Active Resistance not only forms a shelter, but it also creates a state of protection sufficient to seat groups drafting alternative political scenarios. And to create a state within a state, it allows the development of a pocket insurgency that establishes a schism and provides for the development and reception of an autonomous zone.

At the end of the G20 summit in November 2011, and for the first time in history, over four hundred outraged protestors united under Gandhi's slogan "be the change you want to see in the world," installing tents in situ under La Grande Arche of La Defense. The Trêve Hivernale (literally the "Winter Respite," a French law providing exemption from wintertime eviction) does not apply to textile shelters.

WALLED CITY

ISRAEL-PALESTINE

Inhabiting the Walls - Creating Spontaneous Community Spaces

In the Israeli-Palestinian caesura, political institutions no longer envisage the possibility of peace. Interestingly, even during the most active period in the Israeli-Palestinian conflict, only the "peace process" was discussed; the semantics sum up the distance from peace itself. Solutions have to be found by spontaneous non-governmental organizations taking direct action, avoiding processes.

It is in this spirit that Studio Malka developed Walled City, a logical follow-up to the Self-Defense project in Paris. This project stems from *Utopies Croisées*, Malka's book of conversations and projects with the late architect Yona Friedman.

Walled City offers a space of reunification, a link between territories and peoples, beyond borders or religions. This linear city is installed on the West Bank separation wall, from Hebron to Jenin via Bethlehem and Jerusalem.

This so-called security barrier was built in 2002 in the West Bank, and declared an illegal entity and a violation of international law by decision of the International Court of Justice in 2004.

In reaction to oppression and with the desire to create an alternative scenario to current policies, the Pocket of Active Resistance (PAR) is a spontaneous structure, offering a new system of life and resistance, a permanent state of dissent and insurrection.

As this linear bridge city is made up of modular units, the PAR allows the community to grow rapidly by unifying not only local but also international activists and protagonists for peace.

Walled City provides an intervention on this 450-mile-long structure in order to create a safe zone, allowing a sufficient state of protection to allow forums and assemblies that generate alternative political scenarios.

The aim is to first pacify the thickness of this wall and then inhabit this no-man's-land, beyond the walls that separate people, then inhabit the area, and gradually bring peace to the entire region.

The PAR pushes further the Self Defense project as it is a state within the state, an insurrectionary pocket that aims to establish a necessary schism and provide shelter in order to develop an autonomous zone.

Walled City offers an "alter-socius," a political solution in the sense of Politeia, which refers to the constitution of a community. The separation wall becomes a space of unified common resistance, a link between human beings creating a self-proclaimed and self-regulated independent pacifist nation in reaction to the extremist policies and fundamentalist ideologies that plague the region.

PONT9

PARIS I FRANCE

Inhabiting the Bridges - Mobile City

In response to mass production, the economic crises, and the segregation caused by real-estate prices, this structure not only co-opts impoverished or outlying spaces, but also upscales places.

The "lower rungs" of the population can rise more than forty-nine feet above ground, via a system of pylons and interconnected footbridges.

This nomadic micro-city is organized around multiple activities that include residences, offices, and meeting rooms, as well as art galleries, recording studios, shops, playgrounds, restaurants, and nightclubs, all run by the residents themselves.

The structure consists of a modular system, footbridges, and public spaces, all mounted on scaffolding. This moving metropolis can be easily and quickly disassembled and can be adapted to various urban configurations developed according to the number of residents.

It is an organized community of ideas, a hood built from an appropriation of land both conquered and controlled.

BOW-HOUSE

HEERLEN I NETHERLANDS

Inhabiting the Walls—Vertical Public Housing

"*The world is yours*" as Queens rapper Nas once dropped. Literally, what's outside is ours to share. The redefinition of public space as the negative image of private space broadens the range of possibilities in terms of reinterpreting urban space.

These are the guidelines of this hip hop-rooted architecture: to reclaim neglected areas of the city in order to transform them, using existing objects just like a sampler to rebuild a whole new track. Settled as an extension of a public square, the Bow-House showcases a unique kind of shelter. Indeed, this project is an open housing unit, literally a straight continuity of the public space, open to all passers-by and welcoming everyone in a light and clear space. It extends out toward the sidewalks. This spontaneous community location redefines the perception of housing, as it is a shelter for all to share.

Bow-House is a flexible system, not a mobile house, but light and static, zero-cost housing for nomadic people.

Housing, in its essence, is no more than a prime shelter; however, it has turned into an emotional closet; we are collecting objects to "improve" our privacy by filling the empty spaces of our homes.

We could easily find all the services that a house offers in any city: a hotel rather than a bedroom, a spa instead of a shower, a restaurant instead of a kitchen, etc... By making use of the many opportunities that any city provides, we can increase options and lower prices.

The Bow-House project is a wall extension of the property parcel that adds another layer to the existing building. It becomes an eye-opener added to a blind wall, a large bow window added as an extension of the existing building. The house consists of a combination of assembled salvaged windows. As the living memory of buildings to which they once belonged, the windows are assembled and reassembled in a random patchwork—shapes, colors of glass, and types; inward- or outward-opening systems; sliding, pivoting, louvered, or folding windows: the combination of different windows creates a modular screen.

This project aims to encourage public participation as an act of resistance against the laws of the marketplace, the commodification of construction, and the lobbying by local authorities who poison architecture with their standards and labels.

Graffiti and blind walls have always made amazing combinations as they show architectural anatomies that are natural extensions of the public domain. This project presents the background wall perfectly as an urban wallpaper for the house, a welcoming place.

Bow-House is a "graffitectural" installation, an emerging hip hop architecture project that turns the neglected parts of the city into a spontaneous piece, an invitation welcoming everyone who passes down the street.

03

OFF THE GROUND

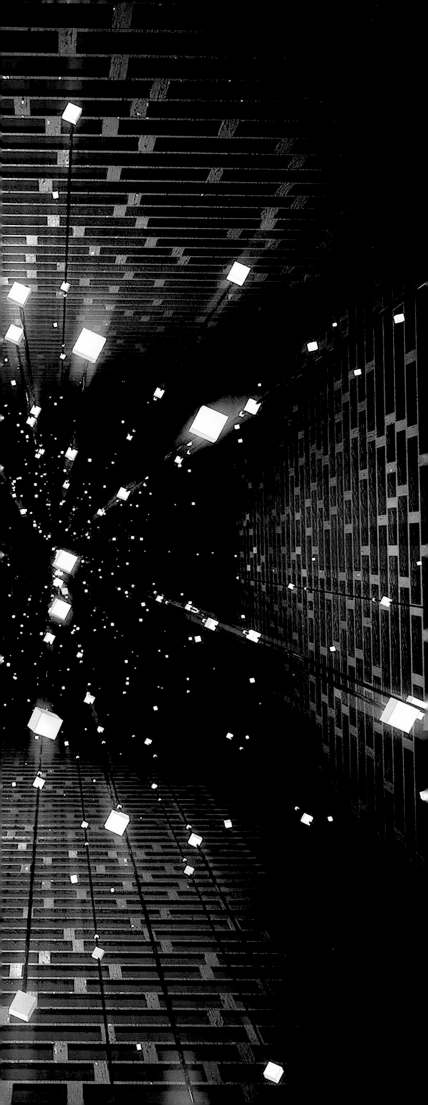

ARDENT CHAPEL

PARIS I FRANCE

Investing the Cathedrals - Inviting Renewal and Tolerance

"Therefore go and make disciples of all nations, baptizing them in the name of the Father and of the Son and of the Holy Spirit, and teaching them to obey everything I have commanded you. And surely I am with you always, to the very end of the age." (Matthew 28:19-20)

In this project, Notre-Dame's Ardent Chapel is a memorial to those persecuted by religious fanaticism and blind proselytizing, from the propagation of religious ideologies to the cultural shock caused by the destruction of the Twin Towers on 9/II. Located on kilometer zero, the base for measuring roads in France, the towers of the memorial rise beyond the duty of memory. They symbolize a desire for renewal and for a less dogmatic religion as well as greater tolerance.

Luminescent urns are suspended in both towers to remind us of the unfortunate fate of religious totalitarianism.

The original plans for Notre-Dame show two spires rising above the towers. After the cathedral was completed in the late twelfth century, it underwent several transformations, including those in the nineteenth century under the supervision of Eugène Viollet-le-Duc. According to the architect, "To restore an edifice means neither to maintain it, nor to repair it, nor to rebuild it; it means to reestablish it in a finished state, which may in fact never have actually existed at any given moment."

Built of simple blocks and planks of wood, traces of the edifice stand upon the bases of the two towers of the cathedral of Notre-Dame. A delicate extension humbly outlining the silhouette of a memorial, it is barely perceptible from the banks of the Seine.

As a light construction without mass, permeable to wind and rain, the memorial connects to Paris and its citizens both visually and physically.

Every night, in both towers, the urns take on a celestial dimension, illuminating the cloudy skies of Paris with a star-studded composition.

3BOX

PARIS I FRANCE

Investing the Roofs - Lowering the market prices

Located on the edge of the river Seine in Paris, these housing units are now possible thanks to "La Loi Alur," new legislation that allows vertical urban expansion. They do not require any lot acquisition as the rights to build are obtained in exchange for the creation of a common area as part of the existing building's renovation. We were therefore able to propose green housing costing forty percent below market price, built offsite and thereby causing minimal disruption, in an extremely short timeframe thanks to our patented panels and unique technique of prefabrication.

These patents were achieved with our team of engineers and specialists. These "energy plus" houses are modular systems that can be extended depending on the user's needs.

Building on top of roofs is not only an ecological and economical solution, but it also prevents the urban sprawl that adversely affects society. It's also a contemporary way to discover new perspectives of the city, a new Paris above the horizon.

MODULAR FOLLIES

MONTPELLIER I FRANCE

Optimizing the Roofs with Mobile Metabolic Architecture

Located in Montpellier's city center in southern France, the Modular Follies aims to be a major landmark building aims to revitalize the neighborhood.

Its claimed goal? Create an alternative location with self-managed habitats and hubs, giving birth to a new iconic and cultural destination. All nested in an ultra-ecological and innovative architecture, built without destroying the existing site or impacting the soils of adjacent construction.

The eight-story high vertical extension takes as its starting point a historical nineteenth-century building, preserved and structurally reinforced.

The Modular Follies is an avant-garde project both in its architectural approach and its programmatic use. It mixes co-living solutions with shared spaces such as libraries, kitchens, restaurants, coffeeshops, a hotel, a cultural hub with exhibition spaces, immersive exhibition halls, suspended gardens, and outdoor recreation areas.

This not a building in the traditional sense of the term, as it actually superimposes several constructions synthesized within a single plot. It would be more appropriate to define it as a vertical village; a superposition of several fragments of urban components with its own streets, businesses, activities and housing on almost all floors.

Each module is invested with one or more functions, as for individual or shared housing capsules, fully equipped, wired and with furniture integrated into the structure, completely ready for use. Entirely prefabricated in local workshops for a clean, fast and nuisance-free construction site, the capsules are flexible and modular, allowing the building to be enlarged over time.

All materials used, including the metallic facade, have been upcycled, refurbished, and refinished as new.

The result is a mobile metabolic eco-architecture, built without tabula rasa or polluting high-tech escalation.

The Modular Follies is also respectful of the site and the existing, both heritage in its preservation of the historic building on which it stands, and fundamentally contemporary in its hybrid approach.

Why is it a Folly? This project is not a real estate project, it is a mobile, living, organic structure, combining architecture and urban planning, community life and culture open to all; The Modular Follies are built on a flexible and extensible structure, allowing an organic development process, thus transforming the morphology of the Follies as new occupants and their modules arrive and leave.

STATION SERVICE

PARIS I FRANCE

Reclaiming the Urban Infill Sites

This project is a vertical extension built on top of an existing gas station, filling the gap in a neglected urban zone to provide habitats connected with studios for artists from diverse disciplines. Station Service is a low-cost building with very low rent income needed, aiming to host emerging talent for various timeframes. It offers studio space and an exhibition space, resulting in a multidisciplinary laboratory showcasing a specifically French creative scene.

The project includes a recording studio, screening room, artists' studios, writers studios, and art gallery, film studio, concert hall, nightclub, and even micro-housing.

Gas stations are the ultimate symbol of architecture's International Style; relocatable at will, they remain identical whether in a suburb of Stockholm, the Arizona desert, or downtown Nairobi.

The facade consists of membranes which provide privacy while powering the building; they are upcycled insulated flexible plastic ducts covering the ventilation and electrical systems cables, connecting the facade to the interior spaces. At the same time, their movement expands and contract the ducts, making muscles in perpetual motion on the facade.

3BOX 92

BOULOGNE-BILLANCOURT | FRANCE

Inhabiting the Roofs - Stacking and Sustainability

Located in Boulogne Billancourt (District 92), west of Paris, 3Box 92 is a two-story vertical extension constructed on a nineteenth-century building. Entirely built with prefabricated systems, the units are stacked on one another, creating mass superpositions, voids, and double heights.

This building is entirely sustainable and has been made with natural and recyclable materials. Its wooden structure is certified from responsibly managed forests and was built in our workshop, causing minimal disruption at the site, and in an extremely short timeframe thanks to our patented panels and unique techniques of prefabrication. These patents were achieved by our team of engineers and specialists.

Moreover, the structure is flexible, built with systems allowing the housing to grow according to the needs of the inhabitants. These systems incorporate panels and high-performance insulation, creating excellent thermal results.

On site, connected modules can be assigned to the most basic needs of architecture such as solar exposition. This concept shapes the volumes and the openings as well as the treatment of the units; the south facade, open toward the garden, is treated with white limewash; its thick walls, double-height spaces, terraces, pool, and cantilevers optimize solar input, thermal inertia, and natural airflow, concepts borrowed from Mediterranean architecture.

Each room is treated like a hotel suite, compact and functional.

The north facade, overlooking the street, is covered with black limewash; on this side, there are spaces which don't require permanent heating or solar input. Made with very few openings, this facade is treated with custom shade systems and shutters to preserve privacy.

Located at the crossroads of hyper-contextual and bicephalous architecture, this project is a contemporary reinterpretation of vernacular Mediterranean architecture, and conveys the complexities of this culture between land and sea.

MID-NITE

IVRY SUR SEINE | FRANCE

Inhabiting the Roofs by Hybridizing the Iconic

This Parisian project is a total refurbishment of an existing building with a new vertical extension.

Paris offers a rich panorama of roofs, most made of zinc, as it is low cost and quick to install. Some were made of copper, as seen in Le Grand Palais or L'Opera Garnier's emblematic oxidized green roofs. The fusion of these two materials create brass, which is the main component of this project.

This alloy is both material and symbolic, a hybridization of Paris's iconic visual identity.

Durable, fully recyclable, and indefinitely reusable, all the materials used were sourced after several generations of recycling.

This project is minimal and radical, consisting of two blocks: a black basement and a golden crown.

Juxtaposed, these two brutally superimposed masses contrast and unite in their own materiality; the pure and deep black block sits on the ground, absorbing and dissolving the light, while the golden and reflective rectangle levitates above.

Mid-Nite is a direct reference to the midnight sun or polar day, during which the sun does not set, both in the North Pole and in the South Pole; indeed, Mid-Nite is an architectural entity in perpetual brilliance, an alliance of the sun and the soil.

During the day the gold block radiates, while it also perpetually illuminates the night in the presence of Paris's famous lamp posts.

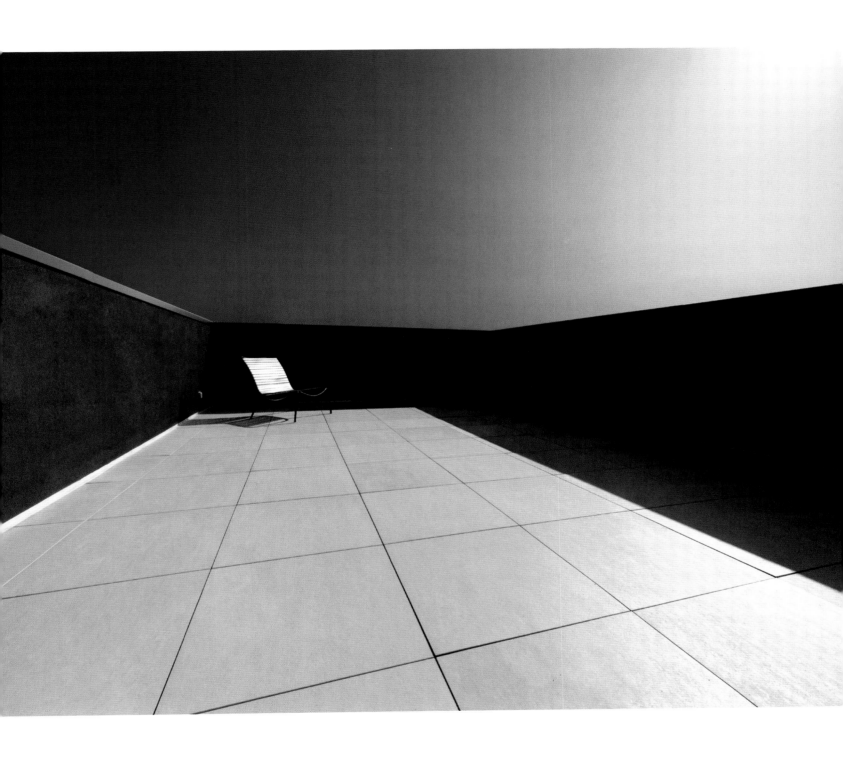

FRENCH EMBASSY

VIENNA I AUSTRIA

Crowning the Roofs

The new French Embassy in Vienna is located at 2 Technikerstraße, within two art nouveau buildings from the beginning of the twentieth century, with an art nouveau identity. These two buildings required refurbishment and a vertical extension both modern and respectful of the site's historic background.

The architectural heightening of one of the buildings was logically thought through in the spirit of art nouveau, symbolizing the relationship between France and Austria, both very active in this movement. To follow through, Studio Malka developed a light and modular extension, prefabricated in our workshop and installed onsite. In this twenty-first-century art nouveau project, rhythms and curved shapes inspired by nature are not used as ornamentation but in the service of its architecture; these modular extensions are circular light cannons. Originally developed in ancient Egypt, this system collects, amplifies, and diffuses natural light in the entire building, while also creating natural ventilation. More than a century after its debut, the new French Embassy in Vienna reconnects with art nouveau's fundamental DNA, while at the same time placing the project in the contemporary architectural landscape.

AME-LOT

PARIS I FRANCE

Reclaiming the Facades

In the construction field, even "green" buildings often generate an over-production of materials, becoming energy-vores and clients of factories, the main polluters of the world.

An important way to combat this is by the reappropriation of materials and experimentations with ready-made objects.

This student housing on Paris's rue Amelot is a project slipped into an urban interstice: the thickness of a blind wall. It is within the thickness of these walls that this thin building is constructed.

The form is a pure geometrical extension of the blind wall; no buildings are destroyed, and no pollution generated.

The skin consists of an easily upcycled, existing module: the wooden pallet. Held using horizontal hinges, the pallets contract toward the top, allowing privacy or large openings.

The modularity of the various palettes creates varied geometries, which are based on use and constantly regenerated.

The reappropriation of materials recycles the existing without any new additional processing, which would consume energy in production and create byproduct pollution.

A wise environmental approach would consist of mandating preservation, adopting new urban policies forbidding destruction, and encouraging the superimposing of interventions upon our built landscape.

It requires a new land strategy, unreferenced on a parcel, constructed in a de facto "ecology" of means.

PLUG-IN CITY

PARIS I FRANCE

Inhabiting the Facades

Located in the heart of the 16th arrondissement of Paris, a stone's throw away from the Seine River, this building from the 1970s is, like most buildings from this period, not energy efficient, due to the presence of thermal bridges, bad insulation, and old standard windows.

The apartments were small and gloomy, which led the co-owners to ask Studio Malka to optimize the property. Since the Alur Law—which relaxed planning laws, particularly those for rooftops, and introduced rent-stabilization measures—does not allow this building to be raised, we decided to graft the building with a succession of extensions, bow windows, and loggias, as well as an extension of the dwellings on the ground floor and the installation of hanging gardens. Each inhabitant controls the necessary surface area needed for its own development upon request.

The structure of the boxes is made of bio-sourced wood, made from wood particles and chips, which allows both lightness and a great flexibility of use on site. Modular and mounted in a workshop, each cube is directly plugged onto the existing facade of the building.

The accumulation of extensions on the facade divides the energy consumption of the building by four, and places the rehabilitation of this building within the Paris Plan Climat regulations.

The transformation of the building adapts it to the real needs of its inhabitants.

For example, the ground floor apartments extend toward the inner garden, allowing the inhabitants of the second floor to benefit from large private terraces open to the sky. Thus, each cube allows two levels of extensions, one covered and one open in its top floor. Private and common interstitial terraces are thus created by default, in the negative space of the loggias.

Utopia of yesterday, today's architecture: the evolution of cities must be built on existing heritage. Para-siting the city, literally, leaning back against it—healing the wounds of the city and its heritage in a logical transformation. By superposition, addition, and extension of the built heritage, rather than the categorical tabula rasa.

NEOSSMANN

PARIS I FRANCE

Enheightening Existing Architecture

Consisting essentially of Haussmannian architecture, Paris has become a static real-estate park.

In response to Paris's increased densification and poor housing, Neossmann is a proposal for urban "enheightning" dedicated to reducing urban sprawl.

These new aerial parcels, distanced from both noise and olfactory pollution, are excellent answers for the question of housing in Paris. Once the supply becomes greater than the demand, housing prices will again become accessible, reviving the Parisian economy through an influx of new residents.

Resting on fortified load-bearing walls, this project launches housing toward the sky, with a translucent facade prepared in a workshop, consisting of simple printed tarps filled with old clothes and rags to provide insulation. Technical constraints are managed in workshops, while the installation of the modules is achieved through innovative construction methods—such as prefabricated systems—that are much faster than conventional construction.

By day, the fabric allows rays of diffuse light to emanate throughout the interior.

By night, the facade becomes practically opaque, with rays of light radiating toward the city.

Built on the roof, this project is an alternative to the incessant quest for a tabula rasa, while also enabling citizens to access housing by literally providing new perspectives through the creation of a city upon the city.

OXYGEN

PARIS LA DEFENSE I FRANCE

Inhabiting the Royal Axis

OxyGen is the winning project for the development of La Defense's former vineyard. This vertical urbanism project is a door, a physical and visual input coming from the railroad tracks and the banks of Neuilly-sur-Seine. This bow is a reception for Le Grand Parvis's promenade. As La Defense slab is mineral, we proposed to create a wide and generous flower garden connected to new restaurants and surrounded by both open and covered terraces, providing outstanding views to the Seine, the Eiffel Tower, and the Arc de Triomphe. The fully green fifth facade plays an important role, not only in the user's pleasure and flow management, but also because it is noticeable from the towers all around. It is an invitation to visually discover the many public spaces OxyGen has to offer on those two levels. The picturesque suspended gardens offer a landscape in constant evolution, inspired by nineteenth-century gardens; the result is an accumulation of Tivolis with different varieties of bushes and grasses but also many planted areas of different sizes to invite people to shelter from the sun, rain, and wind.

Restaurants and kiosks where entirely prefabricated in workshops and delivered directly to the site, without any noise or pollution for residents, office workers, or surrounding hotels guests.

The architectural and landscape design of the project does not dissociate any element of the site. Instead, an unfiltered experience on two levels is provided.

OxyGen downsizes the vertical approach of La Defense; rather, it is the lowest, more sustainable, and greener architectural building of the slab, offering a recycled bamboo facade facing the steel skyscrapers all around. As a result, much needed intimacy and human scaled is created.

Thus, La Defense's bow is transformed, and a camouflage park is created, a blend between architecture and landscape, with an inhabited bridge open on the Seine: a new cultural site and playground for both La Defense and Paris.

TOP NEST

PARIS I FRANCE

Colonizing the Roofscape

Using simple and rapid construction techniques, Top Nest (Haut-Nid in French) is a deliberate act of conquering virgin urban terrain, colonizing the roofscape for new contemporary uses.

An additional rooftop layer allows new possibilities, redefining the use value of a place. Haut-Nid (read "honi" as in Latin for "outcast," a term chosen for this meaning) is for those who yearn to escape in the space of a moment. After a vertical ascent, the context of the roof offers generous, free horizontal views. This place of privacy generates sensory proximity to the city, its people, and its machines, enriched by the variety of sounds and lights of Paris.

Constructed solely of bent plywood panels, the project was mounted on-site in three days. The form was designed to maximize views of the Parisian landscape and sky, resulting in a three-dimensionally curved object that sits discreetly in white, emphasizing the views of Paris by framing the elusive.

EMPTIES(KY)

SANTORINI I GREECE

Investing Troglodyte Architecture

Empties(ky) is a neologism created with *ky* (kyphoscoliosis peptidase), a cytoskeleton protease necessary for muscular growth of humans, and *empties*, standing for voids and lackings. Greece is the source of myth and art, from the Minoan civilization to its recent economic travails.

Santorini, "the cannibal island," a possible Atlantis, was sunk by its own volcano in the magnificent prototype of Greek tragedies, where Mount Olympus is outcast.

This installation brings a new use to this spontaneous construction in Santorini's rock.

Empties(ky) is a vernacular dialogue, a viral white-on-white installation growing on the walls and ceilings of a cave habitat to come, composed of a single item and then multiplied—a parasite spreading itself to the site.

This zero-tech installation upcycles all the polystyrene chips gathered from among the 245 artists parcels from the International Santorini Biennale.

Commissioned for the International Biennale of Santorini, where it was awarded first prize, Empties(ky) aims to reactivate neglected spaces and turn them into dwellings in the medieval village of Pyrgos, in the heart of the Cyclades.

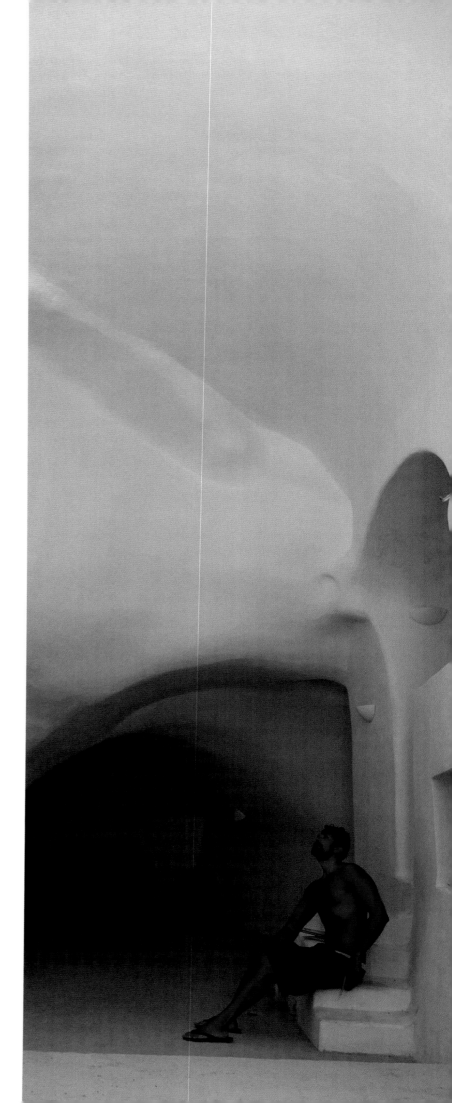

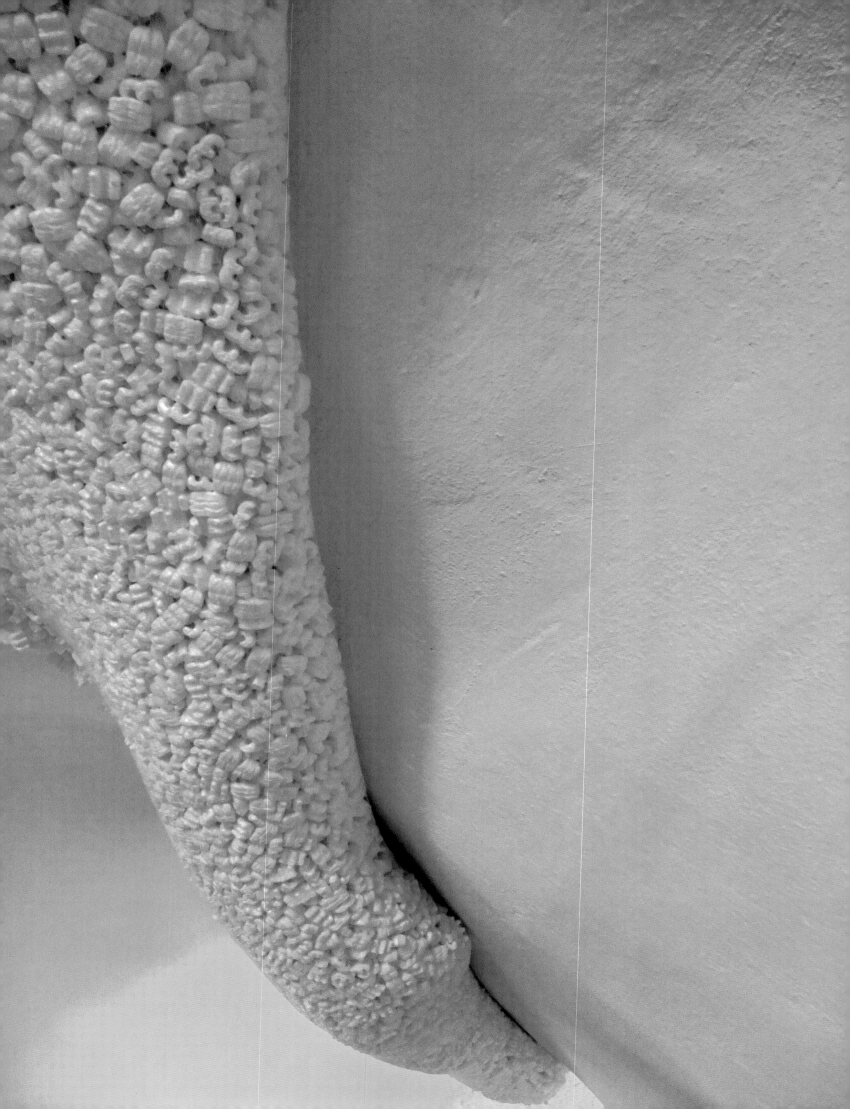

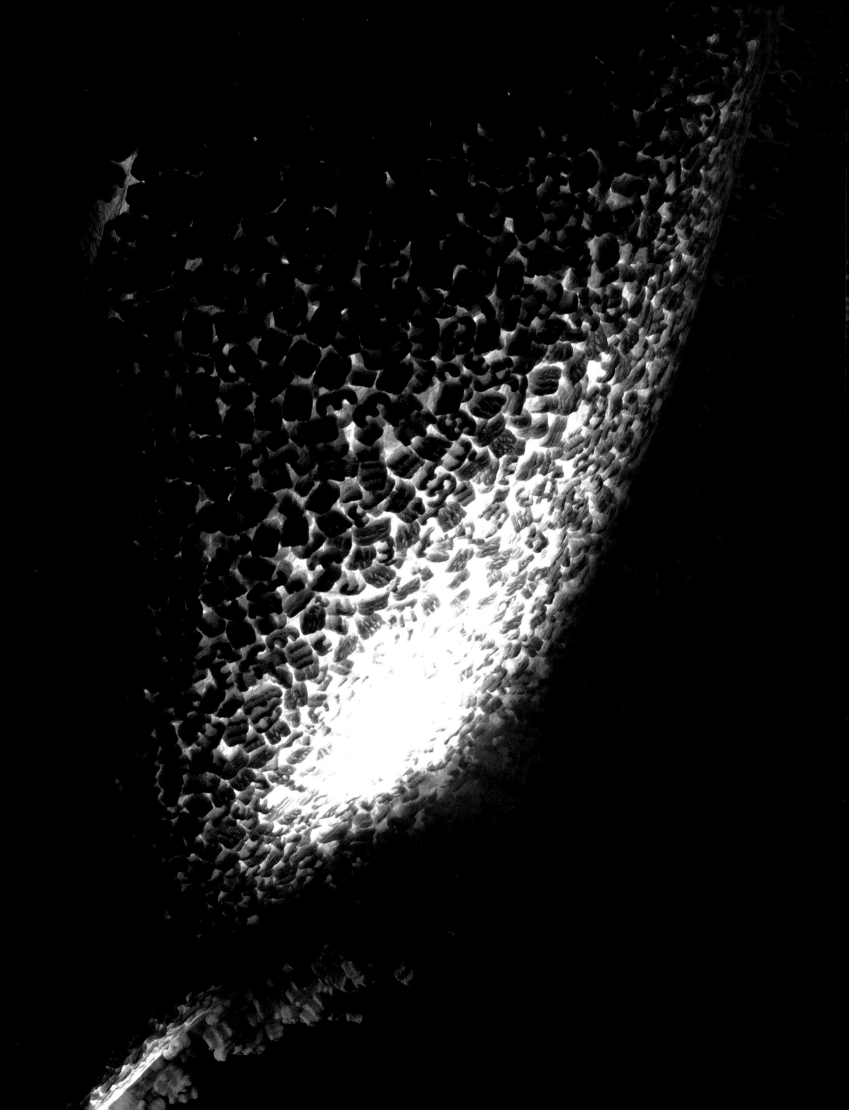

BOOMBOX

MOSCOW I RUSSIA

Architectural Ready-Made
Making Unitary Space from Chaos

Boom (n): onomatopoeia describing the hollow sound of an explosion or a heartbeat. Box (n): a generic container.

Boombox is an installation that envisions the dense city of the future and its habitats.

The approach proposes a projection of the twenty-first century megalopolis through a superposition of boxes representing architectural entities.

The basic module of the installation is the cardboard box.

Appropriated from its original use, it remains a symbol of precarity, containers, and nomadism.

Just like contemporary cities, a unitary space is born from this apparent chaos. The ever-growing city is pushed to the limit; the space is ultra-dense and saturated to its limits. The floor, the walls, and the ceiling are merged together, creating a loss of senses, orientation, and gravity. A mirror reinforces the matrix through multiplicity, pushing the boundaries of perception and creating a spatial abyss.

Cities and graffiti are linked, and here in this installation they merge. They both share systems of proliferation, occupation of space, and appropriation of place.

The result is a total invasion of the space, para-siting the smallest crevices of the site. The space is saturated and supra-tagged, turning the space into a white explosion, sampled and re-transcribed as a three-dimensional equalizer: it's the "X" moment of an urban aspiration, which carries the shouts of the people and of the streets. The brutality of the proliferation contrasts with the softness of the white, creating an ambivalence of senses, an organic introspection in this cosmological space.

This vision of proliferation envisions a futurist megalopolis matrix with an ultra-capitalist urban landscape: the city below, horizontal and proletarian. The vertical cities, middle class, columns between the two cities. The city above, inaccessible, sky's the limit.

BOOMBOX

BARCELONA I SPAIN

At the Crossroads of Art and Architecture

This scenographic installation is a diptych, an extension of the 2010 *No Limits in the Streets* project in Moscow. Boombox is an in situ contextual installation. It programs the dissolution of Santa Monica Art Center and its architecture. This urban installation plays on the dichotomy of its elements; it's a eulogy to cardboard, an inexpensive material symbolizing nomadism, contrasted against stone, a noble material representing longevity in all its static weight. Although separate entities, there is nevertheless an exchange between two bodies, a cultural and social fusion between the academic and the contemporary, at the crossroads between a work of art and a work of architecture. It generates immediate, accessible experiences, highlighting the architectural metamorphosis; the walls are no longer an end in themselves but a blank page on which other interventions can be written, becoming layered and saturated, like graffiti on a wall. BoomBox, evidently the explosion of a box, is also the fragmentation of the building itself and a critique of standardized architecture, a re-transcription of the over-densification of cities and their borders, pushed to a paroxysm. Ground, wall, and ceiling limits are dissolved through the proliferation of cardboard boxes. The laws of gravity do not apply any longer. Our three-dimensional system of reference fades away. This spatial and temporal disorientation creates a new relationship with space, where the spectator/citizen observes the super-densification of the city block by block, simultaneously experiencing a global vision of a fractured monolith.

PANAME ART-CAFÉ

PARIS | FRANCE

Breaking the Walls

Located near the Canal Saint-Martin in the center of the city, Le Paname is Paris's most influential and legendary comedy club.

Born in New York and Chicago's urban's neglected zones, comedy clubs had to reclaim those leftovers and turned them into hype alternative spots. Because comedy clubs often originally occupied industrial brick buildings, the brick wall became the background signature of such clubs in the United States, and, soon enough, all around the world. Original and innovative, this contemporary theater typology breaks the traditional "fourth wall," an imaginary line between the actors and the audience, by encouraging performers to address and interact directly with the audience.

Le Paname comedy club has been thought of as the direct descendant of the Italian Renaissance's stage set, which allowed multiple perspectives; a mirror creates a reflection that stretches the stage into endless views. Here, bricks are integral elements of the project, but they are hijacked from the original stand-up classic code as the space bends, expands, twists, and finally dissolves at the very center of the stage, where the comedian stands. It is an accumulation of single bricks rather than a uniform wall, a timeline of a progressive urban chaos, from alignment to total explosion.

Moreover, it is the physical representation of the fourth wall's dissolution, where urbanity explodes and people remain at the center of the stage's vortex.

04

FLEXIBLE FUTURE

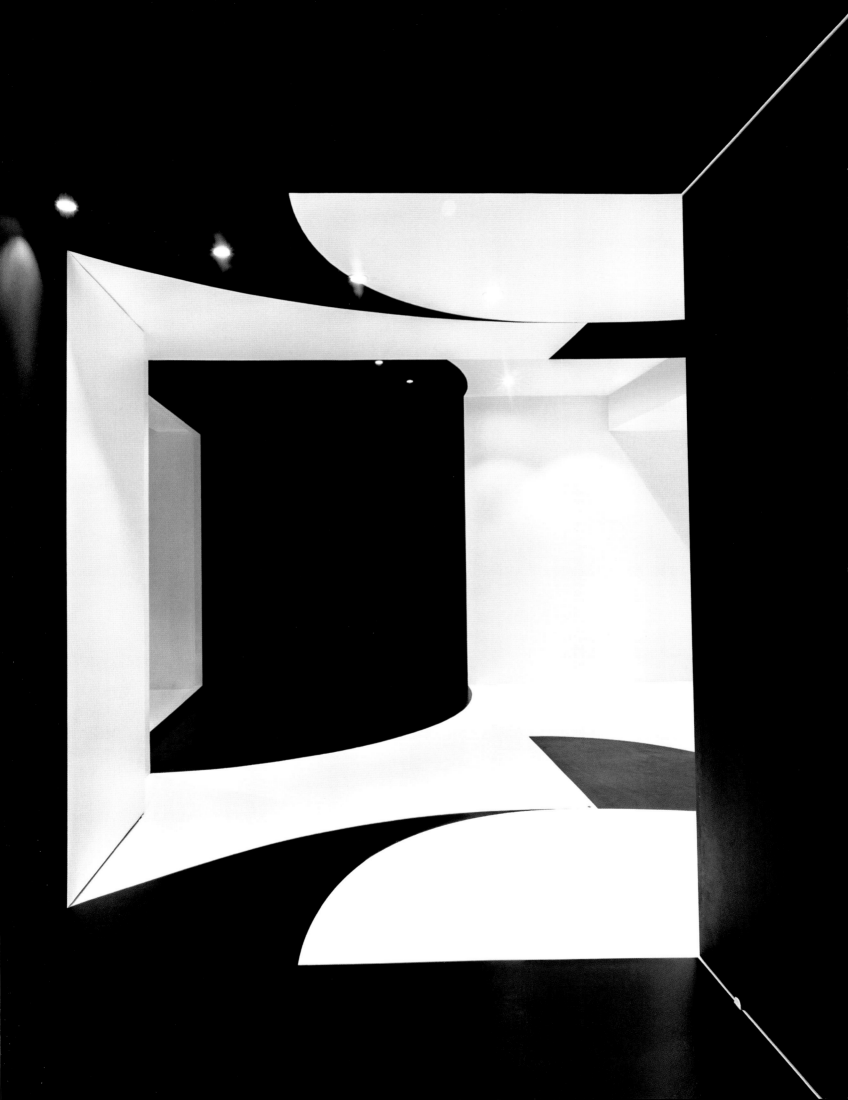

LA NOUVELLE HÉLOïSE

PARIS I FRANCE

Creating Flexible Spaces - Inhabiting Ambiguity

In Paris's 13th arrondissement, a few steps away from the Héloïse and Abélard Square, Studio Malka designed a fully flexible space.
The scope statement mandated a need for multipurpose spaces: an office, a showroom, working spaces, an exhibition space, and living spaces.
To allow this flexibility, we created, developed, and patented floating wall systems, suspended less than a quarter inch above the floor and below the ceiling. These elements that include walls and full height doors are patented under the name of MuMo (Mur Mobiles in French, meaning Mobile Walls).
This system enables multiple combinations of various sizes of spaces. The movement of the MuMo draws multiple axes of rotation; the black and white masses are the results, the physical footprint of this circular motion. The axis intersections are treated like a three-dimensional chessboard, with alternating light and dark cubes.
The result produces a meaningful structure to this ballet of moving walls, where the whole is different from the sum of its parts.
The architecture of La Nouvelle Héloïse materializes a space with multiple ways to discover it, through a flexible and autonomous structural system.
This bicephalous space experiments with visual distortion; false mirrors, symmetries, and real time fish-eye effects. The offices stretch and contract, divide, add, and create polymorphic spaces, from remote workpods to generous meeting-rooms.
The walls glide like musical notes, merely touching each other, hugging and separating perpetually, as a continuous tribute to Héloïse and Abélard.
As a polymorphous space, a monochrome camouflage, the frame of La Nouvelle Héloïse dissolves the space with an ambiguity of its own, somewhere between a familiar space with retro references and the invention of a futuristic typology.

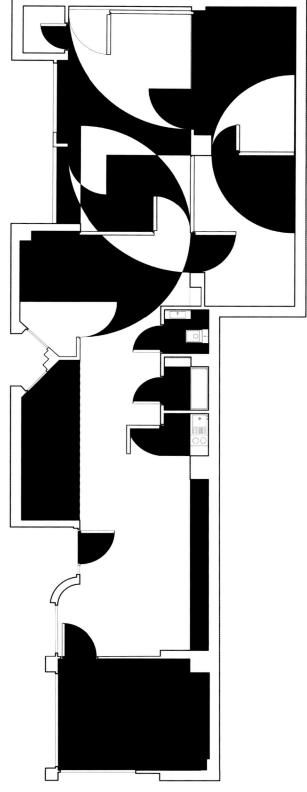

189

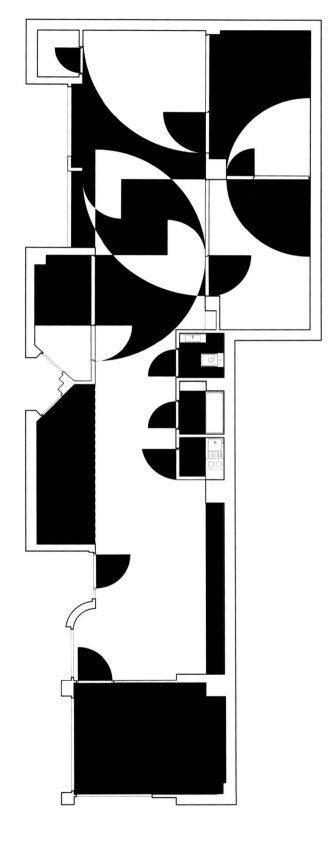

LOUVRE

PARIS I FRANCE

Reclaiming the Museums

Studio Malka was invited to create fifteen modular pavilions inside the historical collection of the Louvre Museum in Paris. These pavilions are designed as extra-small spaces to shelter visitors and invite them to take a break from the rush of the museum. In order to develop adequate micro-architectures within the museum, we began with a systemic analysis.

The arch in all its forms and variations stood out as the Louvre's common architectural denominator, connecting the dots of the various periods of the building's architecture. It is also linked directly to the museum's collections, as the arch is showcased in the Mesopotamian section, and also in the Assyrian, Egyptian, Etruscan, and Roman collections, amongst many others.

The Louvre Pavilions will fit naturally in the Palais Royal's axis, a tribute to L'Arc de Triomphe and La Grande Arche de La Défense. It creates a new connection to Paris's architectural landmarks such as the arcades located on the rue de Rivoli, the iconic bridges of the Seine, and the Eiffel Tower.

Resolutely timeless and yet contemporary, these twenty-first-century arches provide continuity to those already in the Louvre, strengthening the Louvre's fundamental DNA.

Thanks to the different positions possible, since the modules can be connected face to face, back to back, and even at right angles, the Louvre pavilions can adapt perfectly to the geometry of the different galleries of the museum.

The myriad combinations of these modules generate multiple and various geometries, such as successions of arches, vaults, domes, alcoves, and even star-shaped vaults of different heights.

The acoustic system of the arches works like a noise trap, as it absorbs the sounds inside the arches and considerably reduces the sound impact of the room in which the modules are installed. These micro-architectures are built exclusively from various Parisian museum's design leftovers. Entirely prefabricated in workshops, they require only the assembly of the different parts between them on site, resulting in a waste-free and silent construction site.

In a world in pandemic crisis, it is difficult to design a public pavilion without any protocol. No one can predict the impact of virus mutations, or the uses and regulations for public spaces in the future. Also, in this so-called "after-world," we must prepare for various possibilities and create suitable scenarios in order to be able to welcome users in the best possible conditions. This is also why the pavilions are not only modular but also mobile; their positioning and endless combinations can change to ensure social distancing depending on the museum's different needs, especially during peak periods, such as celebrations or school holidays.

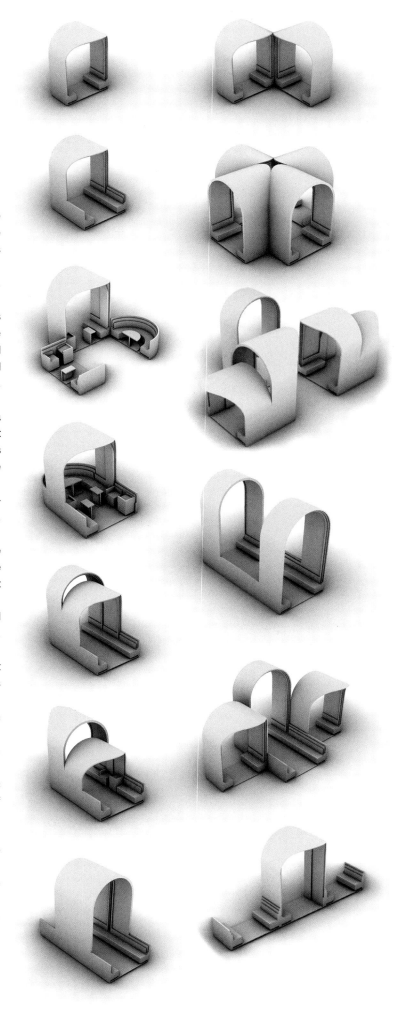

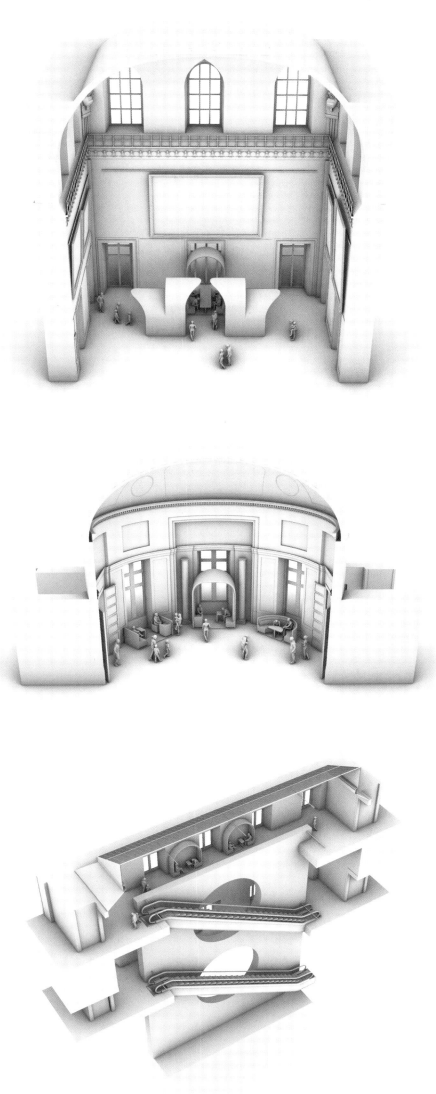

ADYAX

PARIS I FRANCE

Chromatic Architecture

Our work for open-source experts Adyax's Parisian headquarters aims to redefine the concept of space planning and create new ways to live and work together in a twenty-first century office building.

Work spaces are still based on the same model rooted in the industrial era. Now obsolete, they are no longer able to adapt to new ways of working, especially in the digital realm.

The "paperless office," combined with the dematerialization, increase of mobile or remote working and the varying expectation of autonomy and working in teams, the extension of the company, and the emergence of new workplaces work hubs, create many new opportunities.

These developments create new prospects and new fields of exploration. To rethink these types of spaces, we developed multipurpose modular solutions as well as materials and objects that are part of the project.

We also created new dispositions and alternative workspaces. The use of laptops allows true mobility within the office, so there are work areas with various spatial and chromatic characteristics; a varied range of different atmospheres, including shared spaces, meeting rooms, and private work areas.

To provide places for informal exchanges, planned meetings, and different types of public receptions, we concentrated on distorting scale-related uses.

Sliding PVC walls create a microarchitecture partition—with thermal and acoustic insulation—that structures the space and allows the connection or separation of working spaces in a few seconds.

The abstract, colorful touches provide a strong visual identity and a playful air. The central space, similar to a nave, invites meditation on the essence of emptiness, as in the spaces of a cathedral. It also draws the eye toward the center, then to the side, as the variations in light allow the enjoyment of much-needed calm.

This architectural anamorphosis creates matrix cubes that are anchored to the hall's columns, halfway between abstraction and spatial reality. This blue and gold form is an invitation to contemplate, a golden window on a blue ocean, and a mind opener toward other places.

BIG WHITE

PARIS I FRANCE

Inhabiting Possibilities

BIG White is a space devoted to many kinds of events, and is intended to highlight art projects. Multi-use and protean, it is alternatively an exhibition gallery, a pop-up store, and a place to present new product launches.

Lighting is merged into the architecture; these intelligent lighting systems highlight a succession of various size alcoves and create an immersive experience throughout the space's immaterial geometry.

The space is designed through this lightning lines system without walls or separations, allowing multiple possibilities, which constantly renews the relationship with the space: its architecture, its structure, thickness, and its volume—the space is transformed, stretched, or de-limited without these walls or separations.

The design of the space allows infinite variations, thanks to its contemporary and immaculate whiteness.

OGILVY& MATHER

PARIS I FRANCE

Reviving Workspaces of Cummunity

Studio Malka was commissioned by the publicists Ogilvy & Mather to redesign their new headquarters by the Champs-Elysees in Paris. Initially assigned to design the furniture and the creative platform, the studio's mission quickly turned into the full rehabilitation of the entire eighty-thousand-square-foot building.

This project was completed within a short deadline and an extremely tight budget, with all work done in real time on site.

Our work was concentrated mainly around the changes of use, including:

* Inhabited Walls: PVC tubes allow a hanging system for simple layout and easy pinup. The wall extrusions allow seat tubes and micro-perforated light scattering on the trays.

* Workbenches: large worktables incorporate side seats for visitors or informal exchanges.

* Wa-Walls: space-dividing solutions incorporating storage and featuring cross-sectional views and opaque parts.

* Mutant Ground: an informal meeting space featuring polymorphic mobile seating, designed as an extension of the floor. This is a visual transcription of a dense city, where the varied heights of the vivid red cubes recall an urban roofscape and the glass walls on which they rest reference patios open toward the streets. Mutant Ground allows flexible uses depending on needs; the lightweight parts are easy to clip on and off as they create moving landscapes that face the city itself.

Based on the direction of the floor girders, furrows draw prospects in the ceilings, walls crack in eye-catching openings through screens, offices, and meeting rooms. These superficial "Ogilvy red" incisions link the different spaces by offering a cohesive visual identity for the creative community.

BIG OFFICE

PARIS I FRANCE

Inhabiting Alternative Workspaces

Pernod-Ricard, a world leader in the manufacture and distribution of premium wines and spirits, reached out to Studio Malka Architecture to design its new sixteen-thousand-square-foot offices, including renovating and remodeling two different buildings and merging them together.

To further investigate new ways of working, Studio Malka designed limited edition furniture.

The common floor is composed of an amphitheater, a large open kitchen and tasting area, as well as scientific laboratories for formulation, analysis, and prototyping, where new spirits are developed.

With the Pernod Ricard office, Studio Malka Architecture continues to explore MuFu—Mutant Furniture—stretching the possibility of design and merging different uses into limited edition or unique furniture pieces.

In the center of the patio, the flooring is extruded from the ground into a geometrical landscape, creating an amphitheater under the central courtyard of the building. This "mutant" ground features polymorphous seating systems, and an almost ten-foot-long floating dining table for tastings, creating a central meeting place at the nerve center of the main building.

A series of custom-made stealth furniture with mirrored elements stretches and dissolves space; these camouflage systems allow the enlarging of perspectives while at the same time dematerializing them. Therefore, the kitchen and its storage wall disappear to reflect the amphitheater and the central courtyard, emphasizing the perception of the space. This three-dimensional mirror system, assembled on a hollow cube with a twenty-three degree rotation of the walls and ceilings toward the domed skylight to gain natural light, allows a mise en abyme, creating infinite fields of reflection.

More than a fusion of open space and the cloistered office, the Soundproof Open Pods (SOP) are a new office development. This contemporary alternative to usual workspace solutions introduces a unique typology; they are long, soundproof alcoves, allowing to staff to work quietly around the courtyard. SOP is a true hybrid system, combining flexibility and mobility, with complex layering that incorporates an effective sound absorption system which ensures users are acoustically isolated within the same space.

Tables, storage spaces, and shelving are made with upcycled industrial scaffolding diverted from their original use. These modular systems are easily assembled and dismantled to adapt to different users and different needs, creating a constantly renewed geometry. As they populate the walls they create micro-architectural units that are mobile, stackable, and flexible, and open or closed depending on the needs of the office.

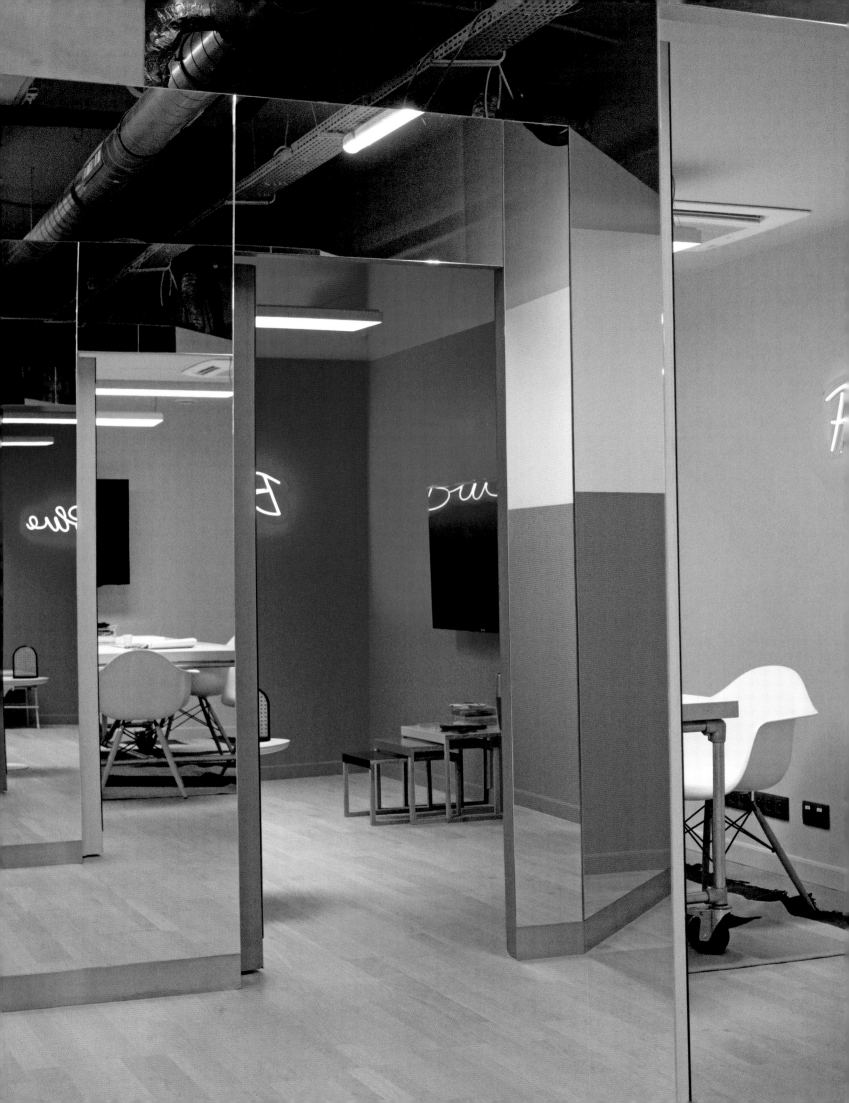

HOMECORE

PARIS I FRANCE

Chromatic Architecture

"*The new architecture permits color organically as a direct means of expressing its relationships within space and time.*"
—Theo Van Doesburg, *Toward a Plastic Architecture*, 1924

Paris-based menswear label Homecore, created in the early 1990s as the first streetwear brand in France, hired Studio Malka to design a brand-new shop on the Champs-Elysèes. This project, inspired by the legendary Krylon logo and Homecore's color therapy concept, is a nod to graffiti and a declaration of esteem to the "peace, love, unity, and having fun" ethos of street culture.

Seven arches define the facade; they are the origin of the chromatic axis that crosses the shop, like drop shadows. The openings are Newton's prisms that disperse white light into the color spectrum. The shop turns into a kaleidoscopic space, a physical representation of the chromatic circle, where vivid tints intersect and add up on each crossing, creating alliances between the masses.

The intersection of each of the arches creates an additive color; red adds to blue to create purple, or to yellow for orange.

Each radiation corresponds to a refractive index, and each intersection is a continued synthesis of the circle where the color transforms itself.

This project gives tangible form to the immaterial space of the spectrum, where color structures the space as a material.

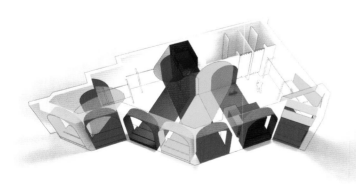

*Huh, you gotta **make somethin' out of nothin'** at all*
I'm sittin' in the classroom learnin' the rules
And it says you can't do graffiti in school
That can't be wrong in the hallowed hall
*So my **notebook turned into a big wall** (...)*
*Still-life **urban masterpiece***
Your trademark was written on trains and walls (...)
*So **learn from the past and work for the future***
And don't be a slave to no computer
Cause the children of man inherit the land
And the future of the world is in your hands

In 1984, the legendary track "Beat Street" was released as part of the soundtrack of the eponymous movie. Performed by Grandmaster Melle Mel & The Furious Five, the song is a retrospective ode to the initiatory journey strewn with pitfalls within hip hop culture, which was then only in its early days.

Two years after that and over three thousand miles away, Stéphane Malka moved from Marseille to Paris, discovering the city and this culture from its depths through his vision as a graffiti artist. Driven by a passionate relationship to urban culture and eager to tap its potential, this respected insider of the vandal crowd invests the smallest corners and porosities of the city in an existential and almost compulsive quest, shot through with danger and adrenaline, transforming the city into both a playground and a battlefield, as he embarked on the ultimate search for beauty while always retaining his survival instinct.

We were then at the dawn of the 1990s, and the millionaire gallery owners were not yet lurking at the edges of street art.

From those rough years when graffiti was confined to a marginal and denigrated subculture, Malka developed a predilection for neglected urban areas in which he saw rich potential. He developed a sensual relationship to the streets, which he loves exploring especially at night. His first street installations were made with upcycled materials, a tribute to what he calls hip hop architecture: to *"make somethin' out of nothin'."*

Years later, as an architect, Stéphane Malka became interested in access to housing for the popular class in which he was born and raised, sharpening his critical eye on the city and its shortcomings, a mixed and supportive background that participated intimately in his architectural awakening.

Architect, designer, theorist, author, and lecturer, Stéphane Malka founded Studio Malka Architecture in 2010 in Paris and opened an office a few years later in Los Angeles an Mallorca. He has collaborated with prestigious international firms such as Ateliers Jean Nouvel, Rem Koolhaas, and Philippe Starck, among others. In 2013, the digital artist Tristan Spella has joined forces with the Studio, bringing a new dimension to Malka's projects. In 2014, he founded "Les Toits du Monde," experts in vertical urban extensions. Also in that year, he published *Le Petit Pari(s)*, a book whose manifesto seeks to reclaim the neglected areas of the city by transforming the rooftops, constructing under bridges, and making the most of the blind facades and various other voids of the city of Paris. Studio Malka Architecture creates unique, ultra-contemporary, innovative avant-garde and conscious architecture in programs as various as housing, office buildings, stage design, installations, and furniture design.

Stéphane Malka's work aims to blend art and architecture in a humanist, positive, and sustainable way. Studio Malka aims to rethink all programs to create new approaches and new uses while bringing innovative solutions to the city. Among his major projects are OxyGen La Défense, Europe's largest business center's new gateway to Paris, the United Nations Cop22 in Marrakech, and Pernod-Ricard's new headquarters in Paris. His projects have been featured in media such as CNN, *Forbes, The Huffington Post, Vogue, Frame, Mark*, and *Architectural Digest*, to name just a few. Multi-awarded by the French Ministry of Culture and the City Hall of Paris, and in 2018 by the international WAN Awards, Malka's works are exhibited around the world in galleries and such museums as the Museum of Modern Art in New York, La Cité de l'Architecture et du Patrimoine in Paris, St. Petersburg's Smolny Sobor, Museum Victoria in Melbourne, Arts Santa Monica in Barcelona, Museum of Design Atlanta, Centre Pompidou-Metz, MuBE and MIS in São Paulo, and the Royal Academy of Arts in London.

CREDITS

07-23 Kheops Observatory.
Program: Observatory, housing, artists residency. Location: Nazlet El Samman, Giza Egypt. Client: Private. Team: Studio Malka. Surface: 450m² Visuals: ©Stéphane Malka 2020

24-27 Golden City.
Program: 250 Student Housing & Embassy reception. Location: Cité Universitaire, Paris France. Client: Egypt Embassy in France. Team: Studio Malka mandatory architects, Associated Consultants, Mercier landscape architects, Laurent Garbit graphist, Betom ingeneers, Alternative Acousticians, Sterling Quest Economists. Surface: 5000 m². Visuals: ©Tristan Spella 2020

28-33 Institut du Monde Arabe.
Program: Temporary installation for "Le Maroc Contemporain" exhibition. Location: Paris, France. Client: Institut du Monde Arabe. Team: Studio Malka, 0+C mandatory architects, Agence du Sud. Surface: 500 m² Surface: 500m². Visuals: ©Laurent Garbit 2014

34-37 COP22's Ark.
Program: Architectural scenography for COP22's United Nations for Climate Change Conference. Location: Marrakech, Morocco. Client: United Nations. Team: Studio Malka, 0+C mandatory architects, GL events, Agence Publics. Surface: 978m² Visuals: ©Laurent Clement 2016

38-49 Mugu House.
Program: Single family housing. Location: Mugu Point Californa, USA. Client: Private. Team: Studio Malka. Surface: 335m². Visuals: ©Tristan Spella 2017

50-55 Casa Lluna.
Program: Single family housing, Working Studios. Location: Mallorca Balearic Islands, Spain. Surface: 280 m². Client: Stephane Malka. Team: Studio Malka, Nora local architects, Patrick Morro apparejador. Surface: 300m². Visuals: ©Stéphane Malka 2023

56-63 Dunk House.
Program: Single family housing. Location: Manhattan Beach California, USA. Client: Private. Surface: 320 m². Team: Studio Malka. Surface: 315m². Visuals: ©Tristan Spella 2019

64-67 Kemer Villas.
Program: Hotel, 78 keys. Location: Kemer, Turkey. Client: Club Med. Team: Studio Malka. Surface: 73 Ha. Visuals: ©Tristan Spella 2015

68-71 Villa Lena.
Program: Hotel extension, yoga studios. Location: Palaia Tuscany, Italy. Client: Villa Lena Foundation. Team: Studio Malka. Surface: 500 Ha. Visuals: ©Tristan Spella 2015

72-73 Bungalow-tech.
Program: Hotel 110 keys. Location: Praslin, Seychelles Islands. Client: Private. Team: Studio Malka, Philippe Starck Netwrok mandatory architects. Surface: 32 Ha. Visuals: ©Tristan Spella 2015

75-79 Loop Camp.
Program: Temporary Camp. Location: Black Rock City Nevada, USA. Client: Black Rock Art Foundation. Team: Studio Malka. Surface: 210m². Visuals: ©Stéphane Malka 2012, page 75; ©NASA World Wind program

80-83 The Green Machine.
Program: Mobile City including housing, agricultural lands, hydroponic agricultural greenhouses, factory. Location: Sahara desert. Client: Binennale Architettura 2014. Team: Studio Malka, Yachar Bouhaya. Surface: 45,000m². Visuals: ©Tristan Spella 2014

84-85 Blvck Pyrvmid.
Program: Basin. Location: Necropolis of Giza, Egypt. Program: Client: Private. Team: Studio Malka. Surface: 57m² Visuals: ©Stéphane Malka 2018

86-91 A-Kamp47.
Program: Vertical Refugee Camp. Location: La Friche de la Belle de Mai Marseille, France. Client: Préavis de Désordre Urbain. Team: Studio Malka. Surface: 2m²/pod. Visuals: ©Laurent Garbit 2013

92-95 Self-Defense.
Program: Pocket of Active Resistance. Location: Grande Arche de la Defense, France. Team: Studio Malka. Surface: Variable. Visuals: ©Michael Kaplan 2009

98-101 Walled City.
Program: Pocket of Active Resistance. Location: Israeli-Plaestinian separation wall. Team: Studio Malka, Yona Friedman consultant. Surface: 45km long. Visuals: ©Tristan Spella 2019

102-107 Pont9.
Program: Ghetto-Mobile. Location: Pont Neuf Paris, France. Team: Studio Malka. Surface: Variable. Visuals: ©Tristan Spella 2014

108-117 Bow-House.
Program: Vertical public house. Location: Heerlen, Netherlands. Client: Cultura Nova - City Liv. Team: Studio Malka. Surface: 95m². Visuals: ©Laurent Clement 2014

119-123 Ardent Chapel.
Program: Memorial. Location: Notre-Dame de Paris Catedral, France. Team: Studio Malka. Surface: 2600m3. Visuals: ©Tristan Spella 2014

124-129 3Box.
Program: Housing. Location: Paris, France. Client: Private. Team: Studio Malka, Les Toits du Monde. Surface: 180m². Visuals: ©Tristan Spella 2016

130-135 Modular Follies.
Program: Co-living, libraries, kitchen, restaurants, coffee shops, hotel, Do Tank cultural hub. Location: Montpellier, France. Client: HPC. Team: Studio Malka. Surface: 1798m². Visuals: ©Tristan Spella 2023

136-139 Station Service.
Program: Co-living, recording studios, screening room, artists and writers studios, art galery, concert hall, night-club. Location: Paris, France. Client: Private. Team: Studio Malka. Surface: 873m². Visuals: ©Tristan Spella 2014

140-145 3Box 92.
Program: Single family house. Location: Boulogne-Billancourt, France. Client: Private. Team: Studio Malka. Surface: 350m². Visuals: ©Stéphane Malka 2018

146-151 Mid-Nite.
Program: Single family house. Location: Ivry sur Seine, France. Client: Jennifer Perez & Thomas Rogé. Team: Studio Malka. Surface: 220m². Visuals: ©Laurent Clement 2019

152-153 French Embassy.
Program: Relocation of services and extension at the French Embassy. Location: Vienna, Austria. Client: Ministry for Europe and Foreign Affairs (France). Team: Studio Malka, Käferhaus Ingineers, Sterling Quest Economists. Surface: 1188m². Visuals: ©Tristan Spella 2022

154-155 Ame-Lot.
Program: Housing extension. Location: Paris, France. Client: Private. Team: Studio Malka . Surface: 615m². Visuals: ©Tristan Spella 2011

156-157 Plug-in City 75.
Program: Extensions of a Housing building. Location: Paris, France. Client: Private. Team: Studio Malka. Surface: Variable. Visuals: ©Tristan Spella 2017

158-161 Neossmann.
Program: Extensions of Housing buildings. Location: Paris, France. Team: Studio Malka. Surface: Variable. Visuals: ©Tristan Spella 2014

162-169 Oxygen.
Program: Refubishment of a vineyard into 4 restaurants, a coffe shop, co-working space, offices and suspended gardens. Client: SAS Oxygen 92—Altarea Cogedim. Location: Paris La Defense, France. Team: Studio Malka, Legendre structural engineers Surface: 120m². Visuals: ©Stéphane Malka 2019

170-171 Top Nest.
Program: Coffee shop. Location: Paris, France. Client: Egon Ellenberg. Team: Studio Malka. Surface: 120m². Visuals: ©Stéphane Malka 2003

172-175 Empties(ky).
Program: Installation- 1st prize winner of the biennale. Location: Santorini Cyclades, Greece. Client: The Santorini Biennale of Arts. Team: Studio Malka. Surface: 120m². Visuals: ©Stéphane Malka 2012

176-177 BoomBox.
Program: Art Installation. Location: Moscow, Russia. Client: International Moscow Biennale. Team: Studio Malka. Surface: 190m². Visuals: ©Michael Kaplan 2010

178-179 BoomBox.
Program: Art Installation. Location: Barcelona, Spain. Client: Eme3 - Arts Santa Monica. Team: Studio Malka. Surface: 180m². Visuals: ©Stéphane Malka 2011

180-183 Paname Art-Café
Program: Stand-Up Comedy Club, restaurant. Location: Paris, France. Client: Le Paname. Team: Studio Malka, GMGB structural engineers. Surface: 260m². Visuals: ©Stéphane Malka 2020

185-195 La Nouvelle Heloïse.
Program: Office,showroom, working spaces, exhibition spaces, living spaces. Location: Paris, France. Client: Agoratic. Team: Studio Malka. Surface: 110m². Visuals: ©Laurent Clement 2016

196-199 Louvre Museum.
Program: 16 Mobile and modular Pavillons. Location: Paris, France. Client: Etablissement Public du Musée du Louvre. Team: Studio Malka, Peutz acoustician, CB économist, Aartil lighting, Citae. Surface: Various. Visuals: ©Tristan Spella 2022

200-207 Adyax.
Program: Adyax headquarters. Location: Paris, France. Client: Adyax Team: Studio Malka mandatory architects, YoonSeux Architects. Surface: 1007m². Visuals: ©Laurent Garbit 2015, page 206-207 ©Laurent Clement 2015

208-213 Big White.
Program: Gallery, showroom. Location: Paris, France. Client: Pernod Ricard. Team: Studio Malka, BTP-consultants control office, Aartil light designers. Surface: 175m². Visuals: ©Laurent Clement 2019

214-217 Ogilvy & Mather.
Program: Ogilvy & Mather's headquarters. Location: Paris, France. Client: Ogilvy & Mather. Team: Studio Malka, BTP-consultants control office, Aartil light designers. Surface: 7 500m². Visuals: ©Laurent Clement & Tristan Spella 2013

218-231 Big Office.
Program: Pernod-Ricard's innovation hub headquarters. Location: Paris, France. Client: Pernod Ricard. Team: Studio Malka, BTP-consultants control office, Aartil light designers. Surface: 1505m². Visuals: ©Laurent Clement 2019

232-237 Homecore.
Program: Shop. Location: Paris, France. Client: Homecore. Team: Studio Malka. Surface: 100 m². Visuals: ©Laurent Clement 2019

Follow Studio Malka online:
Instagram.com/StudioMalka

© 2023 Rizzoli International Publications, Inc.
Text © 2023 Melanie Mendelewitsch
© 2023 Stéphane Malka
Publisher: Charles Miers
Editor: Douglas Curran
Production Manager: Kaija Markoe
Managing Editor: Lynn Scrabis

Designed by Laurent Garbit + Studio Malka
Typography **GROUPE + DNM** © Laurent Garbit

ISBN-13: 978-0-8478-7322-7
Library of Congress
Control Number: 2023935053

Visit us online:
Facebook.com/RizzoliNewYork
Twitter: @Rizzoli_Books
Instagram.com/RizzoliBooks
Pinterest.com/RizzoliBooks
Youtube.com/user/RizzoliNY